THAT WE MIGHT HAVE JOY

HOWARD W. HUNTER

In a general conference address in April 1993, President Howard W. Hunter asked members of The Church of Jesus Christ of Latter-day Saints, "How often do we think of the Savior? How deeply and gratefully and how adoringly do we reflect on his life? How central to our lives do we know him to be?"

Living a more Christlike life has long been a theme of President Hunter's messages to the Saints. *That We Might Have Joy* presents thirty-two of these messages, each expressing his testimony that "Christ's way is not only the *right* way, but ultimately the *only* way to hope and joy."

The book is arranged in four parts: "Making Christ Our Exemplar," "A Plea for Unity," "Facing Trials and Tribulations," and "Becoming Disciples of Christ." Each chapter within these sections draws from the scriptures an important message illustrating how using the Savior's life and teachings as our guide can lead to greater peace of mind and joy.

President Hunter summarizes well this theme in his talk entitled "Facing Trials and Tribulations": "Our task is to have the gospel in our lives and to be a bright light, a city set on a hill, that reflects the beauty of the gospel of Jesus Christ and the joy and happiness that will always come to every people in every age who keep the commandments."

*"These things I speak in the world,
that they might have my joy
fulfilled in themselves."*

(John 17:13)

THAT WE
MIGHT HAVE JOY

Howard W. Hunter

Deseret Book Company
Salt Lake City, Utah

Library of Congress Catalog Card Number 94-68367

ISBN 0-87579-876-4

Printed in the United States of America

10   9   8   7   6   5   4   3   2   1

CONTENTS

CONTENTS

PART 3:
FACING TRIALS AND TRIBULATIONS

PART 4:
BECOMING DISCIPLES OF CHRIST

Part 1

MAKING CHRIST OUR EXEMPLAR

"What manner of men ought ye to be?
Even as I am."
(3 Nephi 27:27)

Chapter 1

"WHAT MANNER OF MEN OUGHT YE TO BE?"

*Let us follow the Son of God in all ways and
in all walks of life. Let us make him our
exemplar and our guide.*

One of the most important questions ever asked of mortal men was asked by the Son of God himself, the Savior of the world. To a group of disciples in the New World, a group anxious to be taught by him and even more anxious because he would soon be leaving them, he asked, "What manner of men ought ye to be?" Then in the same breath he gave this answer: "Even as I am." (3 Ne. 27:27.)

The world is full of people who are willing to tell us, "Do as I say." Surely we have no lack of advice givers on about every subject. But we have so few who are prepared to say, "Do as I do." And, of course, only One in human history could rightfully and properly make that declaration. History provides many examples of good men and women, but even the best of mortals are flawed in some way or another. None could serve as a perfect model nor as an infallible pattern to follow, however well-intentioned they might be.

Only Christ can be our ideal, our "bright and morning star." (Rev. 22:16.) Only he can say without *any* reservation, "Follow me, learn of me, do the things you have seen me do. Drink of my

3

water and eat of my bread. I am the way, the truth, and the life. I am the law and the light. Look unto me and ye shall live. Love one another as I have loved you." (See Matt. 11:29; 16:24; John 4:13–14; 6:35, 51; 7:37; 13:34; 14:6; 3 Ne. 15:9; 27:21.)

My, what a clear and resonant call! What certainty and example in a day of uncertainty and absence of example.

President Ezra Taft Benson said on the subject of Christ's marvelous example (and I add my own witness to the truth of these words), "Nearly two thousand years ago a perfect Man walked the earth—Jesus the Christ. . . . In His life, all the virtues were lived and kept in perfect balance; He taught men truth— that they might be free; His example and precepts provide the great standard—the only sure way—for all mankind." (*Teachings of Ezra Taft Benson* [Salt Lake City: Bookcraft, 1988], 8.)

The great standard! The only sure way! The light and the life of the world! How grateful we should be that God sent his Only Begotten Son to earth to do at least two things that no other person could have done. The first task Christ did as a perfect, sinless Son was to redeem all mankind from the Fall, providing an atonement for Adam's sin and for our own sins if we will accept and follow him. The second great thing he did was to set a perfect example of right living, of kindness and mercy and compassion, in order that all of the rest of mankind might know how to live, know how to improve, and know how to become more godlike.

Let us follow the Son of God in all ways and in all walks of life. Let us make him our exemplar and our guide. We should at every opportunity ask ourselves, "What would Jesus do?" and then be more courageous to act upon the answer. We must follow Christ, in the best sense of that word. We must be about his work as he was about his Father's. We should try to be like him, even as the Primary children sing, "Try, try, try." (*Children's Songbook*, 55.) To the extent that our mortal powers permit, we should make every effort to become like Christ—the one perfect and sinless example this world has ever seen.

His beloved disciple John often said of Christ, "We beheld

4

his glory." (John 1:14.) They observed the Savior's perfect life as he worked and taught and prayed. So, too, ought we to behold his glory in every way we can.

We must know Christ better than we know him; we must remember him more often than we remember him; we must serve him more valiantly than we serve him. Then we will drink water springing up unto eternal life and will eat the bread of life.

What manner of men and women ought we to be? Even as he is.

Chapter 2

"JESUS, THE VERY THOUGHT OF THEE"

Christ's way is not only the <u>right</u> way, but ultimately the <u>only</u> way to hope and joy.

The day that the Christian world traditionally calls Palm Sunday is the anniversary of that momentous occasion nearly two thousand years ago when Jesus of Nazareth, the very Son of God himself, began the ultimate declaration of his divinity and entered the holy city of Jerusalem as the promised Messiah that he was.

Riding on a young donkey in fulfillment of Zechariah's ancient prophecy (see Zech. 9:9), he approached the temple on a path the jubilant crowd lined for him with palm leaves, flowering branches, and some of their own garments, thus carpeting the way properly for the passing of a king. He was their king; these were his subjects. "Hosanna to the Son of David," they shouted. "Blessed is he that cometh in the name of the Lord; Hosanna in the highest." (Matt. 21:9.)

Of course, that path so lovingly lined was soon to lead to an upper room and then to Gethsemane. After stops at the home of Annas, the court of Caiaphas, and the Roman headquarters of Pilate, it would, of course, lead on to Calvary. But it would not end there. The path would lead to the garden tomb and the triumphant hour of resurrection that we celebrate each year on Easter Sunday.

In the lovely springtime season of the year, the annual awakening when, in the northern hemisphere, the world is renewed, blossoms, and turns green and fresh again, we instinctively turn our thoughts to Jesus Christ, the Savior of the world, the Redeemer of mankind, the source of light, and life, and love.

With the rest of the Christian world, the members of The Church of Jesus Christ of Latter-day Saints sing reverently:

> *Jesus, the very thought of thee*
> *With sweetness fills my breast;*
> *But sweeter far thy face to see*
> *And in thy presence rest.*
> —Hymns, *no. 141*

On Palm Sunday and on Easter Sunday, our minds turn very naturally to wonderful thoughts of Jesus. Indeed, Easter, along with perhaps Christmas, may be the only time in the whole year when some of our brothers and sisters in Christ's flock find their way to church. That is admirable, but we wonder if thoughts of Jesus, which "with sweetness" fill our breast, ought not to be far more frequent and much more constant in all times and seasons of our lives. How often do we think of the Savior? How deeply and how gratefully and how adoringly do we reflect on his life? How central to our lives do we know him to be?

For example, how much of a normal day, a working week, or a fleeting month is devoted to "Jesus, the very thought of thee"? Perhaps for some of us, not enough.

Surely life would be more peaceful, surely marriages and families would be stronger, certainly neighborhoods and nations would be safer and kinder and more constructive if more of the gospel of Jesus Christ "with sweetness" could fill our breasts.

Unless we pay more attention to the thoughts of our hearts, I wonder what hope we have to claim that greater joy, that sweeter prize: someday his loving face to see, "and in [his] presence rest."

Every day of our lives and in every season of the year, Jesus asks each of us, as he did following his triumphant entry into Jerusalem those many years ago, "What think ye of Christ? whose son is he?" (Matt. 22:42.)

We declare that he is the Son of God, and the reality of that fact should stir our souls more frequently.

> *Nor voice can sing, nor heart can frame,*
> *Nor can the mem'ry find*
> *A sweeter sound than thy blest name,*
> *O Savior of mankind!*

We testify, as the ancient prophets and apostles did, that the name of Christ is the only name given under heaven whereby a man, woman, or child can be saved. It is a blessed name, a gracious name, a sacred name. Truly no "voice can sing, nor heart can frame, . . . a sweeter sound than [that] blest name."

But even as we should think on the name of Christ more often, and use it more wisely and well, how tragic it is, and how deeply we are pained, that the name of the Savior of mankind has become one of the most common and most ill-used of profanities.

In the Easter season of the year—when we are reminded yet again of all Christ has done for us, how dependent we are upon his redeeming grace and personal resurrection, and how singular his name is in the power to dispel evil and death and save the human soul—may we all do more to respect and revere his holy name and gently, courteously encourage others to do the same. With this lovely hymn as a reminder, let us lift the use of the name of deity to the sacred, sweet elevation that it deserves and that has, indeed, been commanded.

In our own day, as in ancient times, Christ has declared, "Let all men beware how they take my name in their lips. . . . Remember that that which cometh from above is sacred, and must be spoken with care, and by constraint of the Spirit." (D&C 63:61, 64.)

We love the name of our Redeemer. May we redeem it from misuse to its rightful lofty position.

> O hope of ev'ry contrite heart,
> O joy of all the meek,
> To those who fall, how kind thou art!
> How good to those who seek!

What a lovely verse of music, and what a message of hope anchored in the gospel of Christ! Is there one among us, in any walk of life, who does not need hope and seek for greater joy? These are the universal needs and longings of the human soul, and they are the promises of Christ to his followers. Hope is extended to every contrite heart, and joy comes to all the meek.

Contrition is costly: it costs us our pride and our insensitivity, but it especially costs us our sins. For, as King Lamoni's father knew twenty centuries ago, this is the price of true hope. "O God," he cried, "wilt thou make thyself known unto me, and I will give away all my sins to know thee . . . that I may be raised from the dead, and be saved at the last day." (Alma 22:18.) When we too are willing to give away all our sins to know him and follow him, we too will be filled with the joy of eternal life.

And what of the meek? In a world too preoccupied with winning through intimidation and seeking to be number one, no large crowd is standing in line to buy books that call for mere meekness. But the meek shall inherit the earth, a pretty impressive corporate takeover—and done *without* intimidation! Sooner or later, and we pray sooner *than* later, everyone will acknowledge that Christ's way is not only the *right* way, but ultimately the *only* way to hope and joy. Every knee shall bow and every tongue shall confess that gentleness is better than brutality, that kindness is greater than coercion, that the soft voice turneth away wrath. In the end, and sooner than that whenever possible,

9

we must be more like him. "To those who fall, how kind thou art!/How good to those who seek!"

May I affirm as did the author of that ancient hymn:

> *Jesus, our only joy be thou,*
> *As thou our prize wilt be;*
> *Jesus, be thou our glory now,*
> *And thru eternity.*

That is my personal prayer and my wish for all the world. I testify that Jesus is the only true source of lasting joy, that our only lasting peace is in him. I do wish him to be "our glory now," the glory each of us yearns for individually and the only prize men and nations can permanently hold dear. He is our prize in time and in eternity. Every other prize is finally fruitless. Every other grandeur fades with time and dissolves with the elements. In the end we will know no true joy save it be in Christ.

May we be more devoted and disciplined followers of Christ. May we cherish him in our thoughts and speak his name with love. May we kneel before him with meekness and mercy. May we bless and serve others that they may do the same.

Chapter 3

"COME UNTO ME"

We must believe that Jesus Christ can ease
our burdens and lighten our loads.
We must come unto him and there receive
rest from our labors.

In his beloved Galilee, that familiar, favored home region of Jesus, the Son of God not only performed his first recorded miracle but also went on to perform many great miracles that surely must have astonished and awed the people of Galilee who saw them. He healed a leper, cured a centurion's servant, stilled a tempest, cast out devils, healed a paralytic, opened the eyes of the blind, and restored to life a young woman who had died.

Most of the people of his home region would not truly believe. "Is not this Joseph's son?" (Luke 4:22), they asked of Jesus, refusing to acknowledge his divine heritage. Jesus wept over these people who should have known better. Because of their skepticism and unbelief and refusal to repent, he upbraided the cities where most of his mighty works had been done. In severely criticizing and finding fault with the wicked cities of Chorazin, Bethsaida, and Capernaum, he said:

"For if the mighty works, which have been done in thee, had been done in Sodom, it would have remained until this day. But

I say unto you, That it shall be more tolerable for the land of Sodom in the day of judgment, than for thee." (Matt. 11:23–24.)

While anguishing over the wickedness and lack of faith among so many in his home area, the Savior voiced his prayer of gratitude for the humble and plain people who did hear his teachings and did believe. These lowly learners needed him, and they needed his message. They demonstrated that the humble, the needy, and the sorrowing would hear the word of God and cherish it. With reassurance to these new believers and concern for those not choosing to follow him, Christ issued a profound invitation in what Elder James E. Talmage appropriately called "one of the grandest outpourings of spiritual emotion known to man." (*Jesus the Christ* [Salt Lake City: Deseret Book Co., 1949], 258.) These are the words of the Master used in making this appeal:

"Come unto me, all ye that labour and are heavy laden, and I will give you rest. Take my yoke upon you, and learn of me; for I am meek and lowly in heart: and ye shall find rest unto your souls. For my yoke is easy, and my burden is light." (Matt. 11:28–30.)

This invitation and promise is one of the most oft-quoted of all scripture and has been of untold comfort and reassurance to millions. Yet there were those among his hearers that day whose vision was so limited that they could see only a carpenter's son speaking of a wooden yoke, a yoke that, from time to time, he had undoubtedly hewn and shaped from heavy wooden timbers for the oxen of these same men who were listening.

Elder Talmage added: "He invited them from drudgery to pleasant service; from the well-nigh unbearable burdens of ecclesiastical exactions and traditional formalism, to the liberty of truly spiritual worship; from slavery to freedom; but they would not." (*Jesus the Christ*, 259.)

Here was a prophetic appeal and magnificent promise to a troubled people facing great peril, but they could not understand it. He knew what lay ahead for them even if they did not, and he was inviting them to come unto him to find rest and safety for

12

their troubled souls. Had he not already shown them that he could give rest to those who labored with profound illness and disease? Had he not already relieved the burden of those who were heavily laden with sin and the cares of the world? Had he not already raised one from the dead, proving that he possessed the divine power to relieve even that greatest of all universal burdens? And yet most would still not come unto him.

Unfortunately, a refusal to accept his miracles and his glorious invitation is still seen today. This marvelous offer of assistance extended by the Son of God himself was not restricted to the Galileans of his day. This call to shoulder his easy yoke and accept his light burden is not limited to bygone generations. It was and is a universal appeal to all people, to all cities and nations, to every man, woman, and child everywhere.

In our own great times of need we must not leave unrecognized this unfailing answer to the cares and worries of our world. Here is the promise of personal peace and protection. Here is the power to remit sin in all periods of time. We too must believe that Jesus Christ possesses the power to ease our burdens and lighten our loads. We too must come unto him and there receive rest from our labors.

Of course, obligations go with such promises. "Take my yoke upon you," he pleads. In biblical times the yoke was a device of great assistance to those who tilled the field. It allowed the strength of a second animal to be linked and coupled with the effort of a single animal, sharing and reducing the heavy labor of the plow or wagon. A burden that was overwhelming or perhaps impossible for one to bear could be equitably and comfortably borne by two bound together with a common yoke. His yoke requires a great and earnest effort, but for those who truly are converted, the yoke is easy and the burden becomes light.

Why face life's burdens alone, Christ asks, or why face them with temporal support that will quickly falter? To the heavy laden, Christ's yoke gives the power and peace of standing side by side with a God who will provide the support, balance, and the strength to meet our challenges and endure our tasks here in the hardpan field of mortality.

Obviously, the personal burdens of life vary from person to person, but every one of us has them. Furthermore, each trial in life is tailored to the individual's capacities and needs as known by a loving Father in Heaven. Of course, some sorrows are brought on by the sins of a world not following the counsel of that Father in Heaven. Whatever the reason, none of us seems to be completely free from life's challenges. To one and all, Christ said, in effect: As long as we all must bear some burden and shoulder some yoke, why not let it be mine? My promise to you is that my yoke is easy, and my burden is light.

"Learn of me," he said, "for I am meek and lowly in heart." (Matt. 11:29.) Surely the lessons of history ought to teach us that pride, haughtiness, self-adulation, conceit, and vanity contain all of the seeds of self-destruction for individuals, cities, or nations. The ashes and rubble of Chorazin, Bethsaida, and Capernaum are the silent witnesses of the Savior's unheeded warnings to that generation. Once majestic and powerful cities, they no longer exist.

Would we add our names or the names of our families to such a list? No, of course not; but if we would not, we must be truly meek and lowly. By taking the yoke of Jesus upon us and feeling what he felt for the sins of the world, we learn most deeply of him, and we especially learn how to be like him.

President Ezra Taft Benson said, "That man is greatest and most blessed and joyful whose life most closely approaches the pattern of the Christ. This has nothing to do with earthly wealth, power, or prestige. The only true test of greatness, blessedness, joyfulness is how close a life can come to being like the Master, Jesus Christ. He is the right way, the full truth, and the abundant life." (*Ensign*, December 1988, 2.)

The call to come unto him has continued throughout time and is being renewed in our day. Modern scriptures are replete with the same invitation. It is an urgent, pleading call to everyone. Indeed, the calm but urgent appeal is still from the Son of

God himself. He is, in fact, the Anointed One who will lift the greatest of burdens from the most heavily laden. The conditions for obtaining that assistance are still precisely the same. We must come unto him and take his yoke upon us. In meekness and lowliness, we must learn of him in order to receive eternal life and exaltation.

Chapter 4

THE BEACON IN
THE HARBOR OF PEACE

As we search for the shore of safety and peace,
Christ is the only beacon on which
we can ultimately rely.

We are mindful that, in spite of hopeful progress seen in recent years, many parts of the world are still filled with strife and sorrow and despair.

Our hearts are torn and our emotions touched when each day's coverage of local or global news brings yet another story of conflict and suffering and, all too often, open warfare. Surely our prayer is to see the world made a better place in which to live, to see more care and concern for one another, and to see the cause of peace and reassurance increased in every direction and extended to all people.

In the pursuit of such peace and reassurance, may I quote a great voice from the past, President David O. McKay. He said that in order to make the world a better place in which to live, "the first and most important step is to choose as a leader one whose leadership is infallible, whose teachings when practiced have never failed. In [any] tempestuous sea of uncertainty, the pilot must be one who through the storm can see the beacon in the harbor of peace." (*Man May Know for Himself* [Salt Lake City: Deseret Book, 1967], 407.)

The message of The Church of Jesus Christ of Latter-day Saints is that there is but one guiding hand in the universe, only one truly infallible light, one unfailing beacon to the world. That light is Jesus Christ, the light and life of the world, the light that one Book of Mormon prophet described as "a light that is endless, that can never be darkened." (Mosiah 16:9.)

As we search for the shore of safety and peace, whether we be individual women and men, families, communities, or nations, the only beacon on which we can ultimately rely is Christ. He is the one who said of his mission, "I am the way, the truth, and the life." (John 14:6.)

In this age, as in every age before us and in every age that will follow, the greatest need in all the world is an active and sincere faith in the basic teachings of Jesus of Nazareth, the living Son of the living God. Because many reject those teachings, that is all the more reason why sincere believers in the gospel of Jesus Christ should proclaim its truth and show by example the power and peace of a righteous, gentle life.

Consider, for example, this instruction from Christ to his disciples: "Love your enemies, bless them that curse you, do good to them that hate you, and pray for them which despitefully use you, and persecute you." (Matt. 5:44.)

Think what this admonition alone would do in your neighborhood and mine, the communities in which you and your children live, in the nations that make up our great global family. I realize this doctrine poses a significant challenge, but surely it is a more agreeable challenge than the terrible tasks posed for us by the war and poverty and pain the world continues to face.

How are we supposed to act when we are offended, misunderstood, unfairly or unkindly treated, or sinned against? What are we supposed to do if we are hurt by those we love, or are passed over for promotion, or are falsely accused, or have our motives unfairly assailed?

Do we fight back? Do we send in an ever-larger battalion? Do we revert to an eye for an eye and a tooth for a tooth, or, as Tevye

17

says in *Fiddler on the Roof,* do we come to the realization that this finally leaves us blind and toothless?

We all have significant opportunity to practice Christianity, and we should try it at every opportunity. For example, we can all be a little more forgiving. In latter-day revelation the Lord said: "My disciples, in days of old, sought occasion against one another and forgave not one another in their hearts; and for this evil they were afflicted and sorely chastened. Wherefore, I say unto you, that ye ought to forgive one another; for he that forgiveth not his brother his trespasses standeth condemned before the Lord; for there remaineth in him the greater sin. I, the Lord, will forgive whom I will forgive, but of you it is required to forgive all men." (D&C 64:8–10.)

In the majesty of his life and the example of his teachings, Christ gave us much counsel with secure promises always attached. He taught with a grandeur and authority that filled with hope the educated and the ignorant, the wealthy and the poor, the well and the diseased.

His message, as one writer said, "flowed forth as sweetly and as lavishly to single listeners as to enraptured crowds; and some of its very richest revelations were vouchsafed, neither to rulers nor to multitudes, but to the persecuted outcast of the Jewish synagogue, to the timid inquirer in the lonely midnight, and the frail woman by the noonday well." His teachings dealt not so much with ceremony and minutia as with the human soul, and human destiny, and human life filled with faith and hope and charity. "Springing from the depths of holy emotions, [they] thrilled the being of every listener as with an electric flame." In a word, his authority was the authority of God. Christ's voice was pure and pervaded with sympathy. Even the severity of his sternest injunctions was expressed with an unutterable love. (Frederic W. Farrar, *The Life of Christ* [Portland, Oregon: Fountain Publications, 1964], 215.)

Let me recall one of the great stories of Christ's triumph over that which seems to test us and try us and bring fear to our hearts. As Christ's disciples had set out on one of their frequent

18

journeys across the Sea of Galilee, the night was dark and the elements were strong and contrary. The waves were boisterous and the wind was bold, and these mortal, frail men were frightened. Unfortunately there was no one with them to calm and save them, for Jesus had been left alone upon the shore.

As always, he was watching over them. He loved them and cared for them. In their moment of greatest extremity they saw in the darkness an image in a fluttering robe, walking toward them on the ridges of the sea. They cried out in terror at the sight, thinking that it was a phantom that walked upon the waves. And through the storm and darkness, to them—as so often to us, when, amid the darknesses of life, the ocean seems so great and our little boats so small—there came the ultimate and reassuring voice of peace with this simple declaration, "It is I; be not afraid." Peter exclaimed, "Lord, if it be thou, bid me come unto thee on the water." And Christ's answer to him was the same as to all of us: "Come."

Peter sprang over the vessel's side and into the troubled waves, and while his eyes were fixed upon the Lord, the wind might toss his hair and the spray might drench his robes, but all was well. Only when with wavering faith he removed his glance from the Master to look at the furious waves and the black gulf beneath him, only then did he begin to sink. Again, like most of us, he cried, "Lord, save me." Nor did Jesus fail him. He stretched out his hand and grasped the drowning disciple with the gentle rebuke, "O thou of little faith, wherefore didst thou doubt?"

Then safely aboard their little craft, they saw the wind fall and the crash of the waves become a ripple. Soon they were at their haven, their safe port, where all would one day hope to be. The crew as well as his disciples were filled with deep amazement. Some of them addressed him by a title that I declare today: "Of a truth thou art the Son of God." (Adapted from Farrar, *The Life of Christ*, 310–13; see Matt. 14:22–33.)

It is my firm belief that if, as individual people, as families, communities, and nations, we could, like Peter, fix our eyes on

Jesus, we too might walk triumphantly over the swelling waves of disbelief and remain unterrified amid the rising winds of doubt. But if we turn away our eyes from him in whom we must believe, as it is so easy to do and the world is so much tempted to do, if we look to the power and fury of those terrible and destructive elements around us rather than to him who can help and save us, then we shall inevitably sink in a sea of conflict and sorrow and despair.

At such times when we feel the floods are threatening to drown us and the deep is going to swallow up the tossed vessel of our faith, I pray we may always hear amid the storm and the darkness that sweet utterance of the Savior of the world: "Be of good cheer; it is I; be not afraid." (Matt. 14:27.)

Chapter 5

WHERE, THEN, IS HOPE?

*In this world of confusion and rushing,
temporal progress, we need to return
to the simplicity of Christ.*

We live in an interesting period of the history of mankind. The slow pace of man's progress from the beginning gradually commenced to accelerate and gain speed. Today we find advancement moving at such increased momentum that we are often frightened by thoughts of the future. Mankind takes pride in the rapid strides of science that have created conveniences for everyday living. Our health has been improved by the progress of medicine, and our life span has been extended. Sweeping reforms in many areas of society have enhanced our well-being. Business and industry are moving forward at a pace never before known, and this generation has the highest standard of living ever enjoyed by mankind. We are proud to be living in a modern world of achievement.

Will all of this spiraling progress be good for people in the years that lie ahead? Will it be beneficial in every respect to our children and grandchildren? We would agree, no doubt, that many things give us concern. What of the future of the family and home life, which in past generations have been great stabilizing forces in society? What of the solidarity of community and national life? What of the future of our economy, as the consequence of inflation and increased debt? What of the modern course of deterioration of morality and its effect upon individuals, families, nations, and the world? We are forced to admit that what we term as progress brings with it many consequences of serious concern.

We are entering into, or going through, a period of history in which so-called modern thought is taking precedence in the minds of many persons who classify themselves as advocates of a modern generation. The more extreme of these lean toward free thinking and free action without assuming the responsibility people owe to others. Where will we be led if we follow those who advocate freedom of use of drugs and freedom of morality? What will be the result of universal free love, abortions at will, homosexuality, or legalized pornography?

What of spiritual values and the religious ideals of past generations, which have been the great stabilizing influence on society? Modern thinkers claim these have been the great deterrents to people in the freedoms they now seek. There is an effort on the part of so-called modernists to change religious beliefs and teachings of the past to conform to modern thought and critical research. They deemphasize the teachings of the Bible by modern critical methods and deny that scripture is inspired. Modernists teach that Christ is not the Son of God. They deny the doctrine of the atoning sacrifice by which all individuals may be saved. They deny the fact of the resurrection of the Savior of the world and relegate him to the status of a teacher of ethics. Where, then, is hope? What has become of faith?

The Old Testament unfolds the story of the creation of the earth and mankind by God. Should we now disregard this account and modernize the creation according to the theories of the modernists? Can we say there was no Garden of Eden or an Adam and Eve? Because modernists now declare the story of the flood is unreasonable and impossible, should we disbelieve the account of Noah and the flood as related in the Old Testament?

Let us examine what the Master said when the disciples

came to him as he sat on the Mount of Olives. They asked him to tell them of the time of his coming and of the end of the world. Jesus answered: "But of that day and hour knoweth no man, no, not the angels of heaven, but my Father only. But as the days of Noe were, so shall also the coming of the Son of man be. For as in the days that were before the flood they were eating and drinking, marrying and giving in marriage, until the day that Noe entered into the ark, and knew not until the flood came, and took them all away; so shall also the coming of the Son of man be." (Matt. 24:36–39.)

In this statement the Master confirmed the story of the flood without modernizing it. Can we accept some of the statements of the Lord as being true and at the same time reject others as being false?

When Martha heard that Jesus was coming, she went out to meet him, and they discussed the matter of the death of her brother and the resurrection. Jesus said to her, "I am the resurrection, and the life: he that believeth in me, though he were dead, yet shall he live." (John 11:25.)

Both of these statements, the one regarding Noah and the fact of the flood and the one in which he declared himself to be the resurrection and the life, were made by the Lord. How can we believe one and not the other? How can we modernize the story of the flood, or refer to it as a myth, and yet cling to the truth of the other? How can we modernize the Bible and still have it be a guiding light to us and a vital influence in our beliefs?

There are those who declare it is old-fashioned to believe in the Bible. Is it old-fashioned to believe in Jesus Christ, the Son of the Living God? Is it old-fashioned to believe in his atoning sacrifice and the resurrection? If it is, I declare myself to be old-fashioned and the Church to be old-fashioned. In great simplicity, the Master taught the principles of life eternal and lessons that bring happiness to those with the faith to believe.

It doesn't seem reasonable to assume the necessity of modernizing these teachings of the Master. His message concerned principles that are eternal. Following these principles, millions of persons have found rich religious experiences in their lives. People of today's world are seeking a meaningful purpose in life, and thousands are seeking a religious experience that is meaningful. Can such an experience be found in meditation only, or by a seance? Can a meaningful experience be found in trips with drugs or in love-ins? Such an attempt is to go through the back, the side door, or over the wall, not through the way pointed out by the Lord.

When the Lord spoke to the Pharisees at the Feast of the Tabernacles, he used these words: "Verily, verily, I say unto you, He that entereth not by the door into the sheepfold, but climbeth up some other way, the same is a thief and a robber. . . . I am the door of the sheep." (John 10:1, 7.)

A meaningful religious experience can come in no other way than by that door, through the Lord Jesus Christ.

There have always been those who wanted a sign before they would believe. During his ministry the Master was asked on many occasions for a sign.

"The Pharisees also with the Sadducees came, and tempting desired him that he would shew them a sign from heaven. He answered and said unto them, When it is evening, ye say, It will be fair weather: for the sky is red. And in the morning, It will be foul weather to day: for the sky is red and lowring. O ye hypocrites, ye can discern the face of the sky; but can ye not discern the signs of the times? A wicked and adulterous generation seeketh after a sign." (Matt. 16:1–4.)

Perhaps it was with them, as with many today, that truth is not recognized as truth unless it is accompanied by the sensational. What would have been accomplished had the Lord called down thunder and lightning, or plucked a star from the sky, or divided the water to satisfy the curiosity of men? They would probably have said that it was the work of the devil, or that their eyes deceived them.

Signs are evident to the faithful. Sick persons are healed; prayers are answered; changes are wrought in the lives of those who believe, accept, and live the commandments. We prove

Christ by living the principles of his gospel. He made great promises of blessings to those who live the commandments: "I, the Lord, am bound when ye do what I say; but when ye do not what I say, ye have no promise." (D&C 82:10.)

Many of the commandments are restrictive, but reason dictates they are for man's good. In addition to the restrictive commandments are the positive admonitions. The two great imperatives are to love God and love one's fellowmen: "Thou shalt love the Lord thy God with all thy heart, and with all thy soul, and with all thy mind. This is the first and great commandment. And the second is like unto it, Thou shalt love thy neighbour as thyself. On these two commandments hang all the law and the prophets." (Matt. 22:37–40.)

What greater laws could be given to bring peace, prosperity, and progress to people if they will faithfully live the commandments to love?

In this time of rapid change, we can maintain an equilibrium if we preserve a belief in God and a love for him, but we cannot love God unless we love his children also. These are our neighbors, and true love of them knows no class or culture, race, color, or creed.

The members of The Church of Jesus Christ of Latter-day Saints open their arms to neighbors everywhere. The restored Church of Christ assumes its charge and responsibility to take the gospel of Jesus Christ in love to its neighbors over the world and endeavors to help those who receive the gospel to live the teachings of the Master.

In this world of confusion and rushing, temporal progress, we need to return to the simplicity of Christ. We need to love, honor, and worship him. To acquire spirituality and have its influence in our lives, we cannot become confused and misdirected by the twisted teachings of the modernist. We need to study the simple fundamentals of the truths taught by the Master and eliminate the controversial. Our faith in God needs to be real and not speculative. The restored gospel of Jesus Christ can be a dynamic, moving influence, and true acceptance gives us a meaningful, religious experience. One of the great strengths of the Mormon religion is this translation of belief into daily thinking and conduct. This replaces turmoil and confusion with peace and tranquillity.

The Church stands firmly against relaxation or change in moral issues. Spiritual values cannot be set aside, notwithstanding modernists who would tear them down. We can be modern without giving way to the influence of the modernist. If it is old-fashioned to believe in the Bible, we should thank God for the privilege of being old-fashioned.

Chapter 6

WHERE IS PEACE?

*If we look to man and the ways of the world,
we will find turmoil and confusion. If we look
to God, we will find peace for the restless soul.*

On the campus of one of our large universities a few years ago, demonstrating students carried large placards, some of which had the words "We demand peace." It cannot be denied that we live in troubled times and that the lives of most people in the world today are affected by war and unrest. Both sides of the controversy have stated their desire for peace, and politicians talk about an equitable and lasting peace despite the fact that down through history there has been almost continual warfare and political unrest.

The apostle James, in writing to Israel, asked this question: "From whence come wars and fightings among you? come they not hence, even of your lusts that war in your members? Ye lust, and have not: ye kill, and desire to have, and cannot obtain: ye fight and war, yet ye have not, because ye ask not. Ye ask, and receive not, because ye ask amiss, that ye may consume it upon your lusts." (James 4:1–3.)

At the time of this writing, the Jews were revolting against the Romans in defense of their religion and fighting to procure the liberty to which they believed themselves entitled. They had been split in many factions and were having conflicts among themselves. At the same time they were waging wars against the heathens in Egypt, Syria, and other places, killing many and being massacred in turn.

James asks this question: Does not war come from lusts? The Jewish contentions and predatory wars were generated upon lust. Lust has been the motivating force of the wars that have afflicted and desolated the world. One nation has coveted another's territory or property or has attempted to force its will or way of life upon another by resorting to physical violence as a means to accomplish its purposes. Nations kill, slay, burn, and destroy until one of them is overcome. History is a repetitious recital of intentional and wanton destruction of life and property. Today is no different from the yesterdays. The populace prays and cries for peace.

The word *peace* appears frequently in scripture and has many meanings. In classical Greek the word refers to cessation, discontinuance, or absence of hostilities between rival forces. This definition is the antithesis of war and strife. The New Testament, however, has given far wider range of meaning. This is partly due to the influence of the Hebrew word for peace, which is far more comprehensive of meaning. It was commonly used as a form of greeting when persons met or parted: "May peace be with you."

Jesus said, "Daughter, thy faith hath made thee whole; go in peace." (Mark 5:34.)

On the evening of the day of the resurrection, he came to the place where the disciples were assembled and said to them, "Peace be unto you. And when he had so said, he shewed unto them his hands and his side. Then were the disciples glad, when they saw the Lord. Then said Jesus to them again, Peace be unto you." (John 20:19–21.)

Paul has incorporated this greeting into the opening sentences of his letters, as do the other writers of the epistles.

The word has also been used in the New Testament in reference to domestic peace between husband and wife, to harmonious relationships within the whole family, and in many instances to happy, personal relationships with others. It has also been used to mean peace of mind or serenity, and the right relationships between God and man.

Because of differences in definitions, those who seek peace may be searching for unrelated conditions. The peace for which the world longs is a time of suspended hostilities; but people do not realize that peace is a state of existence that comes only upon the terms and conditions set by God, and in no other way.

In a psalm in the book of Isaiah are these words: "Thou wilt keep him in perfect peace, whose mind is stayed on thee: because he trusteth in thee." (Isa. 26:3.) This perfect peace mentioned by Isaiah comes to one only through a belief in God. This is not understood by an unbelieving world.

On the last occasion when Jesus had supper with the Twelve, he washed their feet, broke bread for them, and passed them the cup; then, after Judas had left their midst, the Master spoke to them at some length. Among other things, he told of his impending death and of the legacy he left for each of them. He had accumulated no goods, property, or wealth. The scriptures tell us of no possessions other than the clothing he wore, and on the day of the crucifixion, even that would be divided by soldiers who would cast lots for his coat. His bequest was given to his disciples in these simple yet profound words:

"Peace I leave with you, my peace I give unto you: not as the world giveth, give I unto you. Let not your heart be troubled, neither let it be afraid." (John 14:27.)

He used the Jewish form of salutation and benediction: "My peace I give unto you." This salutation and bequest was not to be taken by them in the usual sense, for he added, ". . . not as the world giveth, give I unto you." Not empty wishes, not just polite ceremony, as the people of the world use the words as matters of custom; but as the Author and Prince of peace, he gave it to them. He bestowed it upon them and said, "Let not your heart be troubled, neither let it be afraid." Within a few hours they would be subjected to trouble, but with his peace they could overcome fear and stand firm.

His last statement to them before the closing prayer on that memorable evening was this: "In the world ye shall have tribulation: but be of good cheer; I have overcome the world." (John 16:33.)

There is no promise of peace to those who reject God, to those who will not keep his commandments, or to those who violate his laws. The prophet Isaiah spoke of the decadence and corruption of leaders and then continued in his admonitions by saying: "The wicked are like the troubled sea, when it cannot rest, whose waters cast up mire and dirt. There is no peace, saith my God, to the wicked." (Isa. 57:21.)

The unrighteous and the wicked have no peace, and their actions take away the peace of others. Turmoil in the world has usually been caused by a few individuals or a minority, causing millions of innocent persons to suffer. Today, as in eras gone by, those who are the innocent victims of oppressors look with hope for peace. This cannot come by riots or placards or even the cessation of hostilities. It can come only in the way the Lord gave his peace to the Twelve, "not as the world giveth."

A great writer named Fenélon said, "Peace does not dwell in outward things, but within the soul; we may preserve it in the midst of the bitterest pain, if our will remains firm and submissive. Peace in this life springs from acquiescence, not in an exemption from suffering." Emerson wrote, "Nothing can bring you peace but yourself; nothing can bring you peace but the triumph of principles." These principles are incorporated into the gospel of Jesus Christ. Indifference to the Savior or failure to keep the commandments of God brings about insecurity, inner turmoil, and contention. These are the opposites of peace. Peace can come to an individual only by an unconditional surrender to him who is the Prince of peace and who has the power to confer peace.

One may live in beautiful and peaceful surroundings, yet, because of inner dissension and discord, be in a state of constant turmoil. On the other hand, one may be in the midst of utter destruction and the bloodshed of war, yet have the serenity of unspeakable peace. If we look to the ways of the world, we will find turmoil and confusion. If we will but turn to God, we will find peace for the restless soul. This was made clear by these words of the Savior: "In the world ye shall have tribulation" (John 16:33); and in his bequest to the Twelve and to all mankind: "Peace I leave with you, my peace I give unto you: not as the world giveth." (John 14:27.)

We can find such peace in a world of conflict if we will but accept his great gift and his further invitation: "Come unto me, all ye that labour and are heavy laden, and I will give you rest. Take my yoke upon you, and learn of me; for I am meek and lowly in heart: and ye shall find rest unto your souls." (Matt. 11:28–29.)

This peace shelters us from the worldly turmoil. The knowledge that God lives, that we are his children, and that he loves us soothes the troubled heart. The answer to the quest lies in faith in God and in his Son, Jesus Christ. This will bring peace to us now and in the eternity to follow.

Chapter 7

THE TEMPTATIONS
OF CHRIST

*Satan continues to tempt, taunt, and plead for
our loyalty. We should take strength from
the fact that Christ was victorious
not as a God but as a man.*

There are times in our struggle with the adversities of mortality when we become weary, weakened, and susceptible to the temptations that seem to be placed in our pathways. A lesson for us lies in the account of the life of the Savior.

Soon after his baptism, Jesus was led by the Spirit into the wild, uncultivated wilderness. There he remained for forty days and nights, preparing himself for the formal ministry that was then to begin. The greatest task ever to be accomplished in this world lay before him, and he needed divine strength. Throughout these days in the wilderness, he chose to fast, so that his mortal body might be completely subjected to the divine influence of his Father's spirit.

When Jesus had completed the fast of forty days and had communed with God, he was, in this hungry and physically weakened state, left to be tempted of the devil. That, too, was to be part of his preparation. Such a time is always the tempter's moment—when we are emotionally or physically spent, when we are weary, vulnerable, and least prepared to resist the

insidious suggestions he makes. This was an hour of danger—
the kind of moment in which many individuals fall and succumb
to the subtle allurement of the devil.

Satan's first temptation was to entice Jesus to satisfy his crav-
ing for food, that most basic, physical, biological need. It was a
temptation of the senses, an appeal to appetite, and in many
ways the most common and most dangerous of the devil's allure-
ments. "If thou be the Son of God," he said, "command that these
stones be made bread." (Matt. 4:3.) During the long weeks of
seclusion, the Savior had been sustained by the exaltation of
spirit that would naturally accompany such meditation, prayer,
and communion with the heavens. In such a devoted spirit,
bodily appetites were subdued and superseded, but now the
demands of the flesh were inevitable.

Satan was not simply tempting Jesus to eat. Had he suggested, "Go down out of this wilderness and obtain food from
the bread maker," there would have been no temptation because
undoubtedly Jesus intended to eat at the close of his fast. Satan's
temptation was to have him eat in a spectacular way—using his
divine powers for selfish purposes. The temptation was in the
invitation to turn stones into bread miraculously, instantaneously, without waiting or postponing physical gratification.
His reply to the tempter was crystal clear: "It is written, Man
shall not live by bread alone, but by every word that proceedeth
out of the mouth of God." (Matt. 4:4.)

Then followed the second temptation. Realizing that he had
utterly failed in his attempt to induce Jesus to use his divine
powers for personal, physical gratification, and having seen
Jesus defer totally to the will and spirit of his Father's sustenance, Satan went to the other extreme and tempted Jesus to
throw himself wantonly upon the Father's protection. He took
Jesus into the Holy City, to the pinnacle of the temple overlook-
ing the spacious courts and people below, and said:

"If thou be the Son of God, cast thyself down: for it is written, He shall give his angels charge concerning thee: and in their

33

hands they shall bear thee up, lest at any time thou dash thy foot against a stone." (Matt. 4:6; see also Ps. 91:11–12.)

There lurked in this appeal from Satan another temptation of the human side of mortal nature: the temptation to perform some dazzling feat, some astounding exploit that might bring crowds of amazed and attentive onlookers. Surely leaping from the dizzying heights of the temple turret and landing in the court-yard unhurt would be such a feat. This would be public recogni-tion that Jesus was a superior being and did have a message from on high. It would be a sign and a wonder, the fame of which would spread like wildfire throughout all Judea and cause many to believe that the Messiah had indeed come. But faith is to pre-cede the miracle; miracles are not to precede the faith. Jesus, of course, answered scripture for scripture by replying, "It is writ-ten again, Thou shalt not tempt the Lord thy God." (Matt. 4:7.) Once more the purposes of Satan were thwarted, and Christ became the victor.

In his third temptation, the devil cast away all subtlety and scripture and all deviousness and disguise. Now he staked everything on a blunt, bold proposition. From a high mountain he showed Jesus all the kingdoms of the world and the glory of them—the cities, the fields, the flocks, the herds, and everything nature could offer. Though they were not his to give, Satan offered them all to Jesus, to him who had lived as a modest vil-lage carpenter.

With wealth, splendor, and earthly glory spread before them, Satan said unto him, "All these things will I give thee, if thou wilt fall down and worship me." (Matt. 4:9.) In a final ploy he was falling back on one of his false but fundamental propositions, one that resulted in his leading astray one-third of the hosts of heaven and that continues to direct his efforts against mankind here on earth. It is the proposition that everyone has a price, that material things finally matter most, that ultimately you can buy anything in this world for money.

Jesus knew that if he were faithful to his Father and obedient to every commandment, he would inherit "all that [the] Father hath" (D&C 84:38)—and so would any other son or daughter of God. The surest way to lose the blessings of time or eternity is to accept them on Satan's terms. Lucifer seemed to have forgotten that this was the Man who would later preach, "For what shall it profit a man, if he shall gain the whole world, and lose his own soul? Or what shall a man give in exchange for his soul?" (Mark 8:36–37.)

In power and dignity, Jesus commanded, "Get thee hence, Satan: for it is written, Thou shalt worship the Lord thy God, and him only shalt thou serve." (Matt. 4:10.) Anguished and defeated, Satan turned and went away. "And when the devil had ended all the temptation," Luke adds, "he departed from him for a season." (Luke 4:13.) Matthew tells us that "angels came and ministered unto him." (Matt. 4:11.)

As with Jesus, so with us, relief comes and miracles are enjoyed after the trial and temptation of our faith. There is, of course, running through all of these temptations, Satan's insidious suggestion that Jesus was not the Son of God, the doubt implied in the tempter's repeated use of the word *if*. "If thou be the Son of God, command that these stones be made bread." (Matt. 4:3.) "If thou be the Son of God, cast thyself down." (Matt. 4:6.) These, of course, foreshadowed that final, desperate temptation which would come three years later: "If thou be the Son of God, come down from the cross." (Matt. 27:40.) But Jesus patiently withstood that ploy also, knowing that in due time every knee would bow and every tongue confess.

It was not necessary then, or ever, for Jesus to satisfy the curiosity of men, least of all unholy men. As victory in every encounter came to Jesus, so the pathos and tragedy of Lucifer's life is even more obvious: first, bold and taunting and tempting; then pleading and weak and desperate; and finally—ultimately—simply banished.

The question for us now is, Will we succeed? Will we resist? Will we wear the victor's crown? Satan may have lost Jesus, but he does not believe he has lost us. He continues to tempt, taunt, and plead for our loyalty. We should take strength for this battle

35

from the fact that Christ was victorious not as a God but as a man.

It is important to remember that Jesus was capable of sinning, that he could have succumbed, that the plan of life and salvation could have been foiled, but that he remained true. Had there been no possibility of his yielding to the enticement of Satan, there would have been no real test, no genuine victory in the result. If he had been stripped of the faculty to sin, he would have been stripped of his very agency. It was he who had come to safeguard and ensure the agency of man. He had to retain the capacity and ability to sin had he willed so to do. As Paul wrote, "Though he were a Son, yet learned he obedience by the things which he suffered" (Heb. 5:8); and he "was in all points tempted like as we are, yet without sin" (Heb. 4:15). He was perfect and sinless, not because he had to be, but because he clearly and determinedly wanted to be. As the Doctrine and Covenants records, "He suffered temptations but gave no heed unto them." (D&C 20:22.)

What about us? We live in a world of temptation—temptation that seems more real and oppressively rampant than any since the days of Noah. Are we remaining faithful in such a world? Every individual in the Church should ask, "Am I living so that I am keeping unspotted from the evils of the world?"

In speaking of the three temptations that came to Jesus, Elder David O. McKay made this statement concerning them: "Classify them, and you will find that under one of those three nearly every given temptation that makes you and me spotted, ever so little maybe, comes to us as (1) a temptation of the appetite; (2) a yielding to the pride and fashion and vanity of those alienated from the things of God; or (3) a gratifying of the passion, or a desire for the riches of the world, or power among men.

"Now, when do temptations come? Why, they come to us in our social gatherings, they come to us at our weddings, they come to us in our politics, they come to us in our business relations, on the farm, in the mercantile establishment, in our dealings in all the affairs of life, we find these insidious influences working, and it is when they manifest themselves to the consciousness of each individual that the defense of truth ought to exert itself." (Conference Report, October 1911, 59.)

Is it just for an individual, or can a body of people withstand the temptations of Satan? Surely the Lord would be pleased with the Saints if they stood before the world as a light that cannot be hidden because they are willing to live the principles of the gospel and keep the commandments of the Lord.

With faith, and prayer, and humility, and sources of strength from an eternal world, we are able to live unspotted in the midst of a world of temptation. With the Psalmist we will sing:

"Yea, though I walk through the valley of the shadow of death, I will fear no evil: for thou art with me; thy rod and thy staff they comfort me.

"Thou preparest a table before me in the presence of mine enemies: thou anointest my head with oil; my cup runneth over.

"Surely goodness and mercy shall follow me all the days of my life: and I will dwell in the house of the Lord for ever." (Ps. 23:4–6.)

Chapter 8

"MASTER, THE TEMPEST IS RAGING"

*It should be no surprise that Jesus could
command a few elements acting up on the Sea
of Galilee. Our faith should remind us that he
can calm the troubled waters of our lives.*

North of Jerusalem about eighty miles or so lies a beautiful
body of water known in biblical times as the Sea of Chinneroth
and the Lake of Gennesaret, but known best to us today as the
Sea of Galilee. It is a freshwater inland lake a little over twelve
miles long and seven miles wide. The river Jordan flows through
it, from north to south, on its journey toward the Dead Sea.

The Sea of Galilee was the lake Jesus knew as a child and a
young man, its western shores lying just twelve or fifteen miles
from his boyhood home of Nazareth. It was to this lake and the
neighboring Galilean hills that Jesus returned so often during
those demanding years of his public ministry.

On one journey to Galilee, the Savior taught the multitudes
crowded near the water's edge. With the people pressing ever
closer, he sought a better teaching circumstance by stepping into
a boat and pushing out a few yards into the sea. There, a short
distance from the eager crowd, he could be seen and heard by
those straining for sight and words of the Master.

Following his discourse, the Savior invited his disciples to join him, and they set out together for the other side of the lake. The Sea of Galilee is quite low, about 680 feet below sea level, and the heat becomes quite great. The hills surrounding the water rise up sharply and to considerable height. The cold air rushing down from the hills meets the warm air rising from the lake in such a way that sudden and temporarily violent storms can occur on the surface of that inland sea. It was just such a storm as this that Jesus and his disciples found as they crossed the lake at evening time. This is the way Mark described it:

"And when they had sent away the multitude, they took him even as he was in the ship. And there were also with him other little ships.

"And there arose a great storm of wind, and the waves beat into the ship, so that it was now full.

"And he was in the hinder part of the ship, asleep on a pillow: and they awake him, and say unto him, Master, carest thou not that we perish?

"And he arose, and rebuked the wind, and said unto the sea, Peace, be still. And the wind ceased, and there was a great calm.

"And he said unto them, Why are ye so fearful? how is it that ye have no faith?

"And they feared exceedingly, and said one to another, What manner of man is this, that even the wind and the sea obey him?" (Mark 4:36–41.)

All of us have seen some sudden storms in our lives. A few of them, though temporary like those on the Sea of Galilee, can be violent and frightening and potentially destructive. As individuals, as families, as communities, as nations, even as a church, we have had sudden squalls arise that have made us ask one way or another, "Master, carest thou not that we perish?" And one way or another we always hear in the stillness after the storm, "Why are ye so fearful? how is it that ye have no faith?"

None of us would like to think we have *no* faith, but I suppose the Lord's gentle rebuke here is largely deserved. This great Jehovah, in whom we say we trust and whose name we have taken upon us, is he who said, "Let there be a firmament in the

39

midst of the waters, and let it divide the waters from the waters." (Gen. 1:6.) And he is also the one who said, "Let the waters under the heaven be gathered together unto one place, and let the dry land appear." (Gen. 1:9.) Furthermore, it was he who parted the Red Sea, allowing the Israelites to pass through on dry ground. (See Ex. 14:21–22.) Certainly it should be no surprise that he could command a few elements acting up on the Sea of Galilee. And our faith should remind us that he can calm the troubled waters of our lives.

Let me recall for you the story of Mary Ann Baker. Her beloved and only brother suffered from the same respiratory disease that had taken their parents' lives, and he left their home in Chicago to find a warmer climate in the southern part of the United States.

For a time he seemed to be improving, but then a sudden turn in his health came, and he died almost immediately. Mary Ann and her sister were heartbroken. It only added to their deep grief that neither their own health nor their personal finances allowed them to claim their brother's body or to finance its return to Chicago for burial.

The Baker family had been raised as faithful Christians, but Mary's trust in a loving God broke under the strain of her brother's death and her own diminished circumstances. "God does not care for me or mine," Mary Ann said. "This particular manifestation of what they call 'divine providence' is unworthy of a God of love." Does that sound at all familiar?

"I have always tried to believe on Christ and give the Master a consecrated life," she said, "but this is more than I can bear. What have I done to deserve this? What have I left undone that God should wreak His vengeance upon me in this way?" (Ernest K. Emurian, *Living Stories of Famous Hymns* [Boston: W. A. Widdle Co., 1955], 83–85.)

I suppose we have all had occasion, individually or collectively, to cry out on some stormy sea, "Master, carest thou not that we perish?" And so cried Mary Ann Baker.

But as the days and the weeks went by, the God of life and

love began to calm the winds and the waves of what this sweet young woman called "her unsanctified heart." Her faith not only returned but it also flourished; and like Job of old, she learned new things, things "too wonderful" to have known before her despair. On the Sea of Galilee, the stirring of the disciples' faith was ultimately more important than the stilling of the sea, and so it was with her.

Later, as something of a personal testimonial and caring very much for the faith of others who would be tried by personal despair, she wrote the words of the hymn we have all sung, "Master, the Tempest Is Raging." May I share it with you:

> *Master, the tempest is raging!*
> *The billows are tossing high!*
> *The sky is o'ershadowed with blackness.*
> *No shelter or help is nigh.*
> *Carest thou not that we perish?*
> *How canst thou lie asleep*
> *When each moment so madly is threat'ning*
> *A grave in the angry deep?*
>
> *Master, with anguish of spirit*
> *I bow in my grief today.*
> *The depths of my sad heart are troubled.*
> *Oh, waken and save, I pray!*
> *Torrents of sin and of anguish*
> *Sweep o'er my sinking soul,*
> *And I perish! I perish! dear Master.*
> *Oh, hasten and take control!*
>
> *The winds and the waves shall obey thy will;*
> *Peace, be still. Peace, be still.*
> *Whether the wrath of the storm-tossed sea*
> *Or demons or men or whatever it be,*
> *No waters can swallow the ship where lies*
> *The Master of ocean and earth and skies.*

They all shall sweetly obey thy will.
Peace, be still, peace, be still.
They all shall sweetly obey thy will.
Peace, peace, be still.

Too often, I fear, both in the living of life and in the singing of this hymn, we fail to emphasize the sweet peace of this concluding verse:

Master, the terror is over.
The elements sweetly rest.
Earth's sun in the calm lake is mirrored,
And heaven's within my breast.
Linger, O blessed Redeemer!
Leave me alone no more,
And with joy I shall make the blest harbor
And rest on the blissful shore.
—Hymns, *no. 105*

We will all have some adversity in our lives. I think we can be reasonably sure of that. Some of it will have the potential to be violent and damaging and destructive. Some of it may even strain our faith in a loving God who has the power to administer relief in our behalf.

To those anxieties I think the Father of us all would say, "Why are ye so fearful? how is it that ye have no faith?" And, of course, that has to be faith for the whole journey, the entire experience, the fulness of our life, not simply around the bits and pieces and tempestuous moments. At the end of the journey, an end none of us can see now, we will say, "Master, the terror is over. . . . Linger, O blessed Redeemer! Leave me alone no more."

Jesus said, "In the world ye shall have tribulation: but be of good cheer; I have overcome the world." (John 16:33.) On the same occasion, he said, "Peace I leave with you, my peace I give unto you: not as the world giveth, give I unto you." (John 14:27.) Throughout his life and ministry he spoke of peace; and when he came forth from the tomb and appeared unto his disciples, his first greeting was "Peace be unto you." (John 20:19.)

But Jesus was not spared grief and pain and anguish and buffeting. No tongue can speak the unutterable burden he carried, nor have we the wisdom to understand the prophet Isaiah's description of him as "a man of sorrows." (Isa. 53:3.) His ship was tossed most of his life, and, at least to mortal eyes, it crashed fatally on the rocky coast of Calvary. We are asked not to look on life with mortal eyes; with spiritual vision we know something quite different was happening upon the cross.

Peace was on the lips and in the heart of the Savior no matter how fiercely the tempest was raging. May it so be with us— in our own hearts, in our own homes, in our nations of the world, and even in the buffetings faced from time to time by the Church. We should not expect to get through life individually or collectively without some opposition.

One of the wisest of the ancient Romans once spoke a great gospel truth and probably never realized he had done so. Speaking of Roman naval power and the absolute imperative to control the oceans, Cicero said to a military aide, "He who commands the sea has command of everything." Of that I so testify.

"Whether the wrath of the storm-tossed sea or demons or men or whatever it be, no waters can swallow the ship where lies the Master of ocean and earth and skies. They all shall sweetly obey [his] will. Peace, be still."

Part 2

A PLEA FOR UNITY

*"Father, keep through thine own name
those whom thou hast given me, . . .
that they may be one,
even as we are one."*
(John 17:11, 22)

Chapter 9

THAT WE MAY BE ONE

Within the Church there is a constant need for unity, for if we are not one, we are not his.

At the time of the conquest of western Palestine after the death of Moses, the tribes of ancient Israel were united under Joshua. Preparations had been made and orders given for the camp to make ready to cross the Jordan and lay siege to Jericho. Joshua told the people that the Lord would do wonders by drying up the river when the feet of the priests leading the march and bearing the ark of the covenant would touch the water. Just as he had foretold, the waters of the Jordan were miraculously dammed up and they crossed over on dry land.

After the people of Israel had crossed the dry riverbed, the Lord commanded Joshua to select twelve men, one from each tribe, to carry on their shoulders twelve stones from the Jordan and lay them down in the place where they would encamp that night. Then he added, "This may be a sign among you, that when your children ask their fathers in time to come, saying, What mean ye by these stones? Then ye shall answer them, That the waters of Jordan were cut off before the ark of the covenant of the Lord; when it passed over Jordan, the waters of Jordan were cut off: and these stones shall be for a memorial unto the children of Israel for ever." (Josh. 4:6–7.)

Fathers have been leaving memorials for their children, and children have been raising them to their fathers, since time began. On Temple Square in Salt Lake City we have consciously surrounded ourselves with such memorials—the old Nauvoo bell, the Seagull Monument, statues of the Restoration, Thorvaldsen's *Christus,* to name just a few. These serve to unite generation with generation, preserving in a long, unbroken chain the important events of our common heritage.

The passage of time and the growth of our institutions often tend to separate us not only from each other but also from our common purposes. Down through history we have been commanded to construct memorials, or hold Passover feasts, or convene general conferences to preserve the power of our united faith and to remember the commandments of God in achieving our eternal, unchanging goals.

More than monuments and festivals are needed, however, for us to succeed in reinforcing our strength and preserving our unity. In much the same way as Joshua did years ago, the builders of the impressive Washington Monument in Washington, D.C., gathered stones from each of the states of the union and encased them within the interior of that 555-foot obelisk, the tallest masonry building in the world, as a tribute not only to the first president and father of our country, but also to our national unity. Yet, while that monument was in preparation, America entered into the bloodiest, most decisive internal conflict it has ever known. It was, as someone has suggested, a civil war fought over a pronoun—should the United States be referred to as "they" or "it"? Memorials and flags and festivals notwithstanding, the Union was at stake, for as President Abraham Lincoln had earlier warned, using the Savior's own words, "If a kingdom be divided against itself, that kingdom cannot stand. And if a house be divided against itself, that house cannot stand." (Mark 3:24–25.)

However great the need may be for unity within nations, there is even greater need for harmony and interdependence within the worldwide Church of Jesus Christ of Latter-day

Saints. In what a modern-day prophet referred to as "the greatest prayer ever uttered in this world" was recorded by the ancient apostle John in impressive detail as he heard it fall from the lips of the Son of God at the close of the evening after Jesus and his apostles had dined together for the last time:

"Father, the hour is come; glorify thy Son, that thy Son also may glorify thee. . . .

"I have manifested thy name unto the men which thou gavest me out of the world: thine they were, and thou gavest them me; and they have kept thy word. . . . I pray for them: I pray not for the world, but for them which thou hast given me; for they are thine. . . .

"Holy Father, keep through thine own name those whom thou hast given me, that they may be one, as we are. . . . As thou hast sent me into the world, even so have I sent them into the world. . . .

"Neither pray I for these alone, but for them also which shall believe on me through their word; that they all may be one; as thou, Father, art in me, and I in thee, that they also may be one in us: that the world may believe that thou hast sent me.

"And the glory which thou gavest me I have given them; that they may be one, even as we are one." (See John 17.)

Within the Church there is a constant need for unity, for if we are not one, we are not his. (See D&C 38:27.) We are truly dependent on each other, "and the eye cannot say unto the hand, I have no need of thee: nor again the head to the feet, I have no need of you." (1 Cor. 12:21.) Nor can the North Americans say to the Asians, nor the Europeans to the islanders of the sea, "I have no need of thee." No, in this church we have need of every member. We pray, as did Paul when he wrote to the church in Corinth, "that there should be no schism in the body; but that the members should have the same care one for another. And whether one member suffer, all the members suffer with it; or one member be honoured, all the members rejoice with it." (1 Cor. 12:25–26.)

Paul's words are as applicable to us today as they were to the saints at Corinth.

49

As we think of the great growth of the Church, the diversities of tongues and cultures, and the monumental tasks that yet lie before us, we wonder if there is any more important objective before us than to so live that we may enjoy the unifying spirit of the Lord. As Jesus prayed, we *must* be united if the world is ever to be convinced that he was sent by God his Father to redeem us from our sins.

It is unity and oneness that has thus far enabled us to bear our testimony around the globe, bringing forward tens of thousands of missionaries to do their part. More must be done. It is unity that has thus far enabled the Church, its wards and stakes, branches and districts, and members, to construct temples and chapels, undertake welfare projects, seek after the dead, watch over the Church, and build faith. More must be done. These great purposes of the Lord could not have been achieved with dissension or jealousy or selfishness. Our ideas may not always be quite like those who preside in authority over us, but this is the Lord's church, and he will bless each of us as we cast off pride, pray for strength, and contribute to the good of the whole.

By the same token, I know of no stronger weapons in the hands of the adversary against any group of men or women in this church than the weapons of divisiveness, faultfinding, and antagonism. In a difficult period of the Church's history, the Prophet Joseph Smith spoke of the opposition that can hinder the Church when we are not filled with the spirit of support and helpfulness.

"The cloud that has been hanging over us," he said, "has burst with blessings on our heads, and Satan has been foiled in his attempts to destroy me and the Church, by causing jealousies to arise in the hearts of some of the brethren; and I thank my heavenly Father for the union and harmony which now prevail in the Church." (*History of the Church* 2:355.)

Of course, the key to a unified church is a unified soul, one that is at peace with itself and not given to inner conflicts and tensions. Much in our world is calculated to destroy that personal peace through sins and temptations of a thousand kinds.

50

We pray that the lives of the Saints will be lived in harmony with the ideal set before us by Jesus of Nazareth.

We pray that Satan's efforts will be thwarted, that personal lives can be peaceful and calm, that families can be close and concerned with every member, that wards and stakes, branches and districts can form the great body of Christ, meeting every need, soothing every hurt, healing every wound until the whole world, as Nephi pleaded, will "press forward with a steadfastness in Christ, having a perfect brightness of hope, and a love of God and of all men. . . . This is the way; and there is none other way." (2 Ne. 31:20–21.)

For the entire worldwide church, for the great body of Saints to the east and to the west, to the north and to the south, we pray that we may be one.

Chapter 10

THE CHURCH
IS FOR ALL PEOPLE

*The clarion call of the Church is for all
to come to Christ, regardless of their
particular circumstances.*

For fifty-two years I enjoyed the sweet companionship of my dear wife. We are still married, for our marriage was sealed in the holy temple to continue on through eternity. Yet with her passing I became one of that increasing number who currently live on this earth as single members of the Church.

Among those who serve as General Authorities of the Church are some who have been raised in single-parent homes, some who are now single because of the loss of their companion, and others who, following such a loss, have found new relationships of marriage with worthy and loving partners. Some who served as General Authorities have preceded their wives in death, leaving their wonderful wives to once again experience that state of singleness that they left at the altar some years before.

The First Presidency, the Council of the Twelve, and the other leaders here at church headquarters are mindful of those who are single. We constantly pray for their happiness and well-being. We recognize that many have special challenges in their lives, and our hearts and our prayers reach out to them.

The Church is for all members. In acknowledging the single or married state of individual Church members, we hope we are not misunderstood, for our intent is not to stereotype them. All of us, single or married, have individual identities and needs, among which is the desire to be seen as a worthwhile individual child of God.

President Ezra Taft Benson told single members of the Church: "We see you as a vital part of the mainstream body of the Church. We pray that the emphasis we naturally place on families will not make you feel less needed or less valuable to the Lord or to His Church. The sacred bonds of Church membership go far beyond marital status, age, or present circumstance. Your individual worth as a daughter [or son] of God transcends all." (*Ensign*, November 1988, 96.)

The clarion call of the Church is for all to come unto Christ, regardless of their particular circumstances. The Book of Mormon reminds us that the Savior "inviteth all to come unto him and partake of his goodness; and he denieth none that come unto him, black and white, bond and free, male and female; [and, we might parenthetically add, single and married] . . . and all are alike unto God." (2 Ne. 26:33.)

This is the church of Jesus Christ, not the church of marrieds or singles or any other group or individual. The gospel we preach is the gospel of Jesus Christ, which encompasses all the saving ordinances and covenants necessary to save and exalt every individual who is willing to accept Christ and keep the commandments that he and our Father in Heaven have given.

Each commandment given is for our benefit and happiness. To love and serve God and to love and serve his Son, our Savior Jesus Christ, should be our goal. Our focus of attention should be on these two holy beings, and we should worship them with all our heart, might, mind, and strength. We should be engaged in assisting them in their divine purposes of bringing to pass the immortality and eternal life of man. (See Moses 1:39.)

The atonement that Christ wrought was in behalf of every individual. However, each must work out his or her own salvation, for we are not saved collectively. The worthiness of one's friends or family will not save him or her. There must be an individual effort. While it is true that worthy couples will obtain exaltation in the celestial kingdom, each man and each woman sealed in an eternal relationship must be individually worthy of that blessing.

An eternal marriage is composed of a worthy man and a worthy woman, both of whom have been individually baptized with water and with the Spirit; who have individually gone to the temple to receive their own endowments; who have individually pledged their fidelity to God and to their partner in the marriage covenant; and who have individually kept their covenants, doing all that God expects of them. And I hasten to add that no blessing, including that of eternal marriage and an eternal family, will be denied to any worthy individual. While it may take somewhat longer—perhaps even beyond this mortal life—for some to achieve this blessing, it will not be denied.

President Spencer W. Kimball gave us this inspired counsel: "Be assured, too, that all faithful sisters, who, through no fault of their own, do not have the privilege during their second estate [earth life] of being sealed to a worthy man, will have that blessing in eternity. On occasions when you ache for that acceptance and affection which belong to family life on earth, please know that our Father in Heaven is aware of your anguish, and that one day he will bless you beyond your capacity to express." (*Ensign,* November 1979, 103.)

During both his mortal ministry among his flock in the Holy Land and his postmortal ministry among his scattered sheep in the Western Hemisphere, the Lord demonstrated his love and concern for the individual.

In the press of a multitude, he sensed the singular touch of a woman who sought relief for an ailment from which she had suffered for some twelve years. (See Luke 8:43–48.) On another occasion, he saw beyond the narrowly focused prejudice of a condemning crowd and the sin of her who stood accused. Perhaps sensing her willingness to repent, Christ chose to see the worth of the individual and sent her forth to sin no more. (See John 8:1–11.) On another occasion, "he took their little children, *one by one,* and blessed them, and prayed unto the Father for them." (3 Ne. 17:21; italics added.)

As the trials of Gethsemane and Calvary fast approached, with much weighing heavily upon his mind, the Savior took time to notice the widow casting in her mite. (See Mark 12:41–44.) Similarly, his gaze took in the small-statured Zacchaeus, who, unable to see because of the size of those congregating around the Savior, had climbed a sycamore tree for a view of the Son of God. (See Luke 19:1–5.) While hanging in agony upon the cross, Jesus overlooked his own suffering and reached out in caring concern to the weeping woman who had given him life. (See John 19:25–27.)

What a marvelous example for us to follow! Even in the midst of great personal sorrow and pain, our Exemplar reached out to bless others. This was typical of one whose mortal life had known few comforts and who had said, "The foxes have holes, and the birds of the air have nests; but the Son of man hath not where to lay his head." (Matt. 8:20.) His was not a life focused on the things he did not have. It was a life of reaching out in service to others.

How foolish we would be to fail to enjoy the rich gifts of God to us! We could well miss opportunities for providing needed blessings to others because we felt personally deprived of some hoped-for blessing and were blinded by our own self-pity.

Not only should we be careful not to deprive others of blessings because of our wanderings in the wastelands of self-pity or self-recrimination, but we should also be careful not to deprive *ourselves* of other blessings that could be ours.

While waiting for promised blessings, one should not mark time, for failure to move forward is to some degree retrogression. Each of us must be anxiously engaged in good causes, including our own development. The personal pursuit of hobbies or crafts, the seeking of knowledge and wisdom, particularly of the things of God, and the development and honing of skills are all things that could productively occupy our time.

Now, may I offer a few words of counsel and love.

To those who are unmarried men: Don't put off marriage because you are not in a perfect career and financial position. Do not, however, rush into a relationship without proper forethought and inspiration. Prayerfully seek the Lord's guidance on this matter. Stay worthy of receiving that divine assistance. Remember that as a priesthood bearer, you have the obligation to take the lead in seeking eternal companionship.

To those who are unmarried women: The promises of the prophets of God have always been that the Lord is mindful of you; if you are faithful, *all* blessings will be yours. To be without marriage and a family in this life is but a temporary condition, and eternity is a long time. President Benson reminded us that "time is numbered only to man. God has your eternal perspective in mind." (*Ensign,* November 1988, 97.) Fill your lives with worthwhile, meaningful activities.

To those who have experienced divorce: Don't let disappointment or a sense of failure color your perception of marriage or of life. Do not lose faith in marriage or allow bitterness to canker your soul and destroy you or those you love or have loved.

To those who are widowed: The most important part of your life is *not* over. For some, there will be appropriate opportunity for further companionship and remarriage. But for those who, for whatever reason, do not choose this path, there can still be marvelous opportunities in life for personal growth and service to others.

To those who are priesthood and auxiliary leaders: Follow the scriptural counsel to look after the widows and the fatherless. (See D&C 83:6.) Take a prayerful interest in those who are single or in single-parent homes. Help them feel wanted, but not uncomfortably singled out. Remember, the Church is for *all* members.

To each Church member: Practice the pure religion mentioned by the apostle James, which is "to visit the fatherless and widows." (James 1:27.) Be kind and considerate of all members. Be thoughtful. Be careful in what you say. Don't allow an insensitive remark or action to harm another. "And above all things, clothe yourselves with the bond of charity, as with a mantle, which is the bond of perfectness and peace." (D&C 88:125.)

May God bless each of us to treat one another as befits one who refers to himself as a Latter-day Saint. May there be none among us who are made to feel like "strangers and foreigners," but may we all feel like "fellowcitizens with the saints, and of the household of God." (Eph. 2:19.)

Chapter 11

THE GOSPEL:
A GLOBAL FAITH

*The restored gospel is a message of divine love
for all people everywhere.*

The gospel of Jesus Christ, which gospel we teach and the ordinances of which we perform, is a global faith with an all-embracing message. It is neither confined nor partial nor subject to history or fashion. Its essence is universally and eternally true. Its message is for all the world, restored in these latter days to meet the fundamental needs of every nation, kindred, tongue, and people on the earth. It has been established again, as it was in the beginning, to build brotherhood, to preserve truth, and to save souls.

Brigham Young once said about such a broad and stimulating concept of religion: "For me, the plan of salvation must . . . circumscribe [all] the knowledge that is upon the face of the earth, or it is not from God. Such a plan incorporates every system of true doctrine on the earth, whether it be ecclesiastical, moral, philosophical, or civil: it incorporates all good laws that have been made from the days of Adam until now; it swallows up the laws of nations, for it exceeds them all in knowledge and purity; it circumscribes the doctrines of the day, and takes from the right and the left, and brings all truth together in one system, and leaves the chaff to be scattered hither and thither." (*Journal of Discourses* 7:148.)

As members of the Church of Jesus Christ, we seek to bring all truth together. We seek to enlarge the circle of love and understanding among all the people of the earth. Thus we strive to establish peace and happiness, not only within Christianity but among all mankind.

In the message of the gospel, the entire human race is one family descended from a single God. All men and women have not only a physical lineage leading back to Adam and Eve, their first earthly parents, but also a spiritual heritage leading back to God the Eternal Father. Thus, all persons on earth are literally brothers and sisters in the family of God.

It is in understanding and accepting this universal fatherhood of God that all human beings can best appreciate God's concern for them and their relationship to each other. This is a message of life and love that strikes squarely against all stifling traditions based on race, language, economic or political standing, educational rank, or cultural background, for we are all of the same spiritual descent. We have a divine pedigree; every person is a spiritual child of God.

In this gospel view, there is no room for a contracted, narrow, or prejudicial view. The Prophet Joseph Smith said: "Love is one of the chief characteristics of Deity, and ought to be manifested by those who aspire to be the sons of God. A man filled with the love of God, is not content with blessing his family alone, but ranges through the whole world, anxious to bless the whole human race." (*History of the Church* 4:227.)

In 1907, the First Presidency presented to the general conference a declaration that includes this statement: "Our motives are not selfish; our purposes not petty and earth-bound; we contemplate the human race, past, present and yet to come, as immortal beings, for whose salvation it is our mission to labor; and to this work, broad as eternity and deep as the love of God, we devote ourselves, now, and forever." (Conference Report, April 1907, appendix, 16.)

In the gospel view, no person is alien. No one is to be denied. There is no underlying excuse for smugness, arrogance, or pride. Openly scorning the pettiness and intolerance of rival religious groups, the Prophet Joseph Smith said in an editorial:

"While one portion of the human race is judging and condemning the other without mercy, the Great Parent of the universe looks upon the whole of the human family with a fatherly care and paternal regard; He views them as His offspring, and without any of those contracted feelings that influence the children of men, causes 'His sun to rise on the evil and on the good, and sendeth rain on the just and on the unjust.' He holds the reins of judgment in His hands; He is a wise Lawgiver, and will judge all men, not according to the narrow, contracted notions of men, but, 'according to the deeds done in the body whether they be good or evil,' or whether these deeds were done in England, America, Spain, Turkey, or India." (*History of the Church* 4:595–96.)

Mormonism, so-called, is a world religion, not simply because its members are now found throughout the world, but chiefly because it has a comprehensive and inclusive message based upon the acceptance of all truth, restored to meet the needs of all mankind.

We believe there is a spiritual influence that emanates from the presence of God to fill the immensity of space. (See D&C 88:12.) All human beings share an inheritance of divine light. God operates among his children in all nations, and those who seek God are entitled to further light and knowledge, regardless of their race, nationality, or cultural traditions.

Elder Orson F. Whitney, in a conference address, explained that many great religious leaders were inspired. He said: "[God] is using not only his covenant people, but other peoples as well, to consummate a work, stupendous, magnificent, and altogether too arduous for this little handful of Saints to accomplish by and of themselves. . . .

"All down the ages men bearing the authority of the Holy Priesthood—patriarchs, prophets, apostles, and others, have officiated in the name of the Lord, doing the things that he required of them; and outside the pale of their activities other good and great men, not bearing the Priesthood, but possessing profundity of thought, great wisdom, and a desire to uplift their fellows, have been sent by the Almighty into many nations, to give them, not the fulness of the Gospel, but that portion of truth that they were able to receive and wisely use." (Conference Report, April 1921, 32–33.)

The restored gospel is a message of divine love for all people everywhere, based upon the conviction that all humans are children of the same God. This primary religious message was beautifully expressed in a statement of the First Presidency on February 15, 1978, as follows: "Based upon ancient and modern revelation, The Church of Jesus Christ of Latter-day Saints gladly teaches and declares the Christian doctrine that all men and women are brothers and sisters, not only by blood relationship from common mortal progenitors, but also as literal spirit children of an Eternal Father."

Latter-day Saints have a positive and inclusive approach toward others who are not of our faith. We believe that we are all literally brothers and sisters, that we are sons and daughters of the same Heavenly Father. We have a common genealogy leading back to God. But more than that, we also seek the true and the beautiful wherever it may be found. And we know that God has blessed all his children with goodness and light, in accordance with the conditions in which they find themselves.

In our humble efforts to build brotherhood and to teach revealed truth, we say to the people of the world what President George Albert Smith so lovingly suggested: "We have come not to take away from you the truth and virtue you possess. We have come not to find fault with you nor criticize you. We have not come here to berate you because of things you have not done; but we have come here as your brethren . . . and to say to you: 'Keep all the good that you have, and let us bring to you more good, in order that you may be happier and in order that you may be prepared to enter into the presence of our Heavenly Father.'" (In

Sharing the Gospel with Others, comp. Preston Nibley [Salt Lake City: Deseret News Press, 1948], 12–13.)

In summary, then, the validity, the power, of our faith is not bound by history, nationality, or culture. It is not the peculiar property of any one people or any one age. As the Prophet Joseph Smith once said, it is "above the kingdoms of the world." (*History of the Church* 5:526.)

Ours is a perennial religion based on eternal, saving truth. Its message of love and brotherhood is lodged in scripture and in the revelations of the Lord to his living prophet. It embraces all truth. It circumscribes all wisdom—all that God has revealed to man, and all that he will yet reveal. Of that eternal revelation, I bear testimony.

Chapter 12

SECRETLY A DISCIPLE

*We have more respect for one who
honestly doubts than for one
who fears to declare loyalty.*

In the nineteenth chapter of John we read the story of an influential man who was secretly a disciple of Christ but, because of fear, was not openly a disciple. Those who declared themselves as followers of Christ were not popular in Jerusalem during this controversial period. Joseph of Arimathea was secretly a disciple, but his fear of what others might think or do prevented him from declaring his allegiance until after the crucifixion of the Master.

Joseph of Arimathea was a man of wealth and station in Jerusalem. We can assume that he had a wide acquaintance and was a man of influence. He was a member of the Sanhedrin, the assembly of seventy-one men constituting the supreme council of the aristocracy that administered the Jewish law. Because of his membership in this tribunal, he was referred to as "counsellor." He is referred to by Mark as "an honourable counsellor, which also waited for the kingdom of God." (Mark 15:43.) Joseph waited in the background, doing nothing to support or sustain the Master. No doubt he had heard Jesus and listened to his teachings, for we are told that he was a secret disciple of the Savior.

When the council was called into session early in the morning following the Last Supper and the betrayal, Joseph either absented himself from the council or refused to vote. He took no part in the proceedings, hoping no doubt to save his own conscience. He would not lift a finger to condemn the Savior, nor would he defend him openly.

There are many like Joseph of Arimathea, individuals who do not declare loyalty to the Lord Jesus Christ, but merely "wait for the kingdom." Like Joseph, they are secret followers of Jesus and halfhearted, lukewarm Christians. Secret disciples of Christ are almost in the same category as those who are antagonistic. They are much the same as persons among us today who have only a halfhearted interest in our great democratic way of life and are as dangerous to the future freedom of the world as those who are openly avowed to destroy democracy.

We would have greater respect for Joseph if he had taken a strong position in the council and defended Jesus. We cannot assume that this would have changed the judgment or saved him from the cross, because he stated at the supper that he would shortly leave them. Nevertheless, we have respect for one who stands upon moral convictions and upholds the right.

We have more respect for one who honestly doubts than for one who fears to declare loyalty. Thomas doubted. He traveled the path from faith through the valley of doubt to new heights of faith. This is the course that many follow in life. As children we accepted as fact the things that were told to us by our parents or our teachers because of the confidence we had in them. A little boy will jump from a high place without fear if his father tells him that he will catch him. The little fellow has faith that his father will not let him fall. As children grow older, they commence to think for themselves, to question and have doubts about those things that are not subject to tangible proof. I have sympathy for young men and women when honest doubts enter their minds and they engage in the great conflict of resolving doubts. These doubts can be resolved, if they have an honest desire to know the truth, by exercising moral, spiritual, and mental effort. They will emerge from the conflict into firmer, stronger, larger faith because of the struggle. They have gone from a simple, trusting faith, through doubt and conflict, into a solid, substantial faith that ripens into testimony.

The Bible is replete with such examples. We think of Abraham in the Old Testament and Thomas in Christ's time. The record does not indicate to us that Joseph of Arimathea doubted as did Thomas. We are told he was "a disciple of Jesus, but secretly for fear. . . ." (John 19:38.) He believed secretly because he was afraid of public opinion. Among our own people, in our communities, in our nation, and throughout the world, there are secret followers of Jesus and halfhearted Christians—onlookers who have a noncommittal attitude. Why is it that so many will not commit themselves?

Joseph of Arimathea was a secret disciple only because of what others would think of him. He would not risk his social position or the respect of his associates. It is fear that causes people to be noncommittal. They are afraid to declare their loyalty and assume active responsibility. The easy way is to let someone else be the leader and assume the responsibility. The world needs individuals who are willing to step forward and declare themselves. The world needs individuals who will lift the load of responsibility to their shoulders and carry it high under the banner of Jesus Christ—individuals who are willing to defend the right openly. I am always impressed by our missionaries. They are willing to accept the call to serve two years or more at their own expense and give freely of their time without monetary compensation, to cry repentance and declare that Jesus is the Christ. This is the type of devotion to principle that is needed in the world today.

How can people of conscience ignore the teachings of the Master in their daily affairs, in business, or in government? We stand by and wink at many things because we fear to do anything about them. We may be against crime, but what do we do about it? We may be against corruption in government or against juvenile delinquency, but what do we do about it? We may have a belief in the gospel of Jesus Christ, but what are we doing about it? We need to push fear into the background and come forward with a definite, positive declaration, and assume responsibility.

The pathway to exaltation is well defined. We are told to have faith in the Lord Jesus Christ and repent of those things which are not according to his teachings. After this change of mental attitude, and with firm resolution, we must declare ourselves by going into the waters of baptism, thereby making a covenant with the Lord to keep his commandments. Can we thereafter be secret disciples? Can we stand on the sidelines and merely observe? This is a day for action. This is the time for decision, not tomorrow, not next week. This is the time to make our covenant with the Lord. Now is the time for those who have been noncommittal or who have had a halfhearted interest to come out boldly, declare belief in Christ, and be willing to demonstrate faith by works.

We acquire more regard for Joseph of Arimathea as we continue to read. Although he was secretly a disciple of Jesus, and although he was one who "waited for the kingdom of God," yet he was finally moved to action. The account continues: "He went to Pilate, and begged the body of Jesus. Then Pilate commanded the body to be delivered. And when Joseph had taken the body, he wrapped it in a clean linen cloth, and laid it in his own new tomb, which he had hewn out in the rock: and he rolled a great stone to the door of the sepulchre, and departed." (Matt. 27:58–60.)

I wonder if there was not a tear in Joseph's eye as he placed the body of Jesus in the tomb. Surely he thought of the events that had taken place earlier on that day, when, as a member of the council, he had failed to come to the defense of the Master. Should we not search our own souls and inquire of ourselves if we are loyal? Are we too only secret disciples of Christ?

This same Jesus who died on the cross and whose body was placed in the tomb came forth on the third day thereafter. He was resurrected and lives today—the Savior of the world. This is my witness. He stands before us with arms outstretched to our vision, and those same words spoken to the disciples in Jerusalem should ring in our ears:

"If any man will come after me, let him deny himself, and take up his cross, and follow me. For whosoever will save his life shall lose it: and whosoever will lose his life for my sake shall find it." (Matt. 16:24–25.)

Chapter 13

"ALL ARE
ALIKE UNTO GOD"

*As members of the Church, we need to lift
our vision beyond personal prejudices.*

In the Book of Mormon we find the following passage referring to the Lord's relationship to the children of men throughout
the earth: "He inviteth them all to come unto him and partake of
his goodness; and he denieth none that come unto him, black and
white, bond and free, male and female; and he remembereth the
heathen; and all are alike unto God, both Jew and Gentile." (2 Ne.
26:33.)

From this statement it is clear that *all* persons are invited to
come unto him and *all* are alike unto him. Race makes no difference; color makes no difference; nationality makes no difference.

The brotherhood of man is literal. We are all of one blood and
the literal spirit offspring of our eternal Heavenly Father. Before
we came to earth, we belonged to his eternal family. We associated and knew each other there. Our common paternity makes
us not only literal sons and daughters of eternal parentage, but
literal brothers and sisters as well. This is a fundamental teaching
of The Church of Jesus Christ of Latter-day Saints. May I cite several passages from the scriptures that refer to our common paternity and how our nationalities were determined.

First, from Paul's address on Mars Hill to the intellectuals in the marketplace at Athens. Because the people were worshipping an unknown god, Paul directed his remarks to an explanation of the true God. He said: "And [God] hath made of one blood all nations of men for to dwell on all the face of the earth, and hath determined the times before appointed, and the bounds of their habitation." (Acts 17:26.)

The words "hath made of one blood all nations of men" refer to Adam, the mortal father of the nations of men. All human beings descend from one man. Paul said that by divine plan, Adam's offspring were scattered over the earth at "the times before appointed"—that is, the period fixed by God for the several families to go into the countries where he decreed they should dwell. Not only did God determine the times when they should go, but also the "bounds of their habitation"—in other words, the countries where they should dwell so that their posterity might carry out the Lord's divine purposes.

The second passage of scripture is from the Book of Deuteronomy: "When the most High divided to the nations their inheritance, when he separated the sons of Adam, he set the bounds of the people according to the number of the children of Israel." (Deut. 32:8.) This indicates that the Lord separated Adam's offspring into nations and at the same time provided an inheritance for the children of Jacob.

A third passage is this statement made by Peter to Cornelius and his friends: "Of a truth I perceive that God is no respecter of persons: But in every nation he that feareth him, and worketh righteousness, is accepted with him." (Acts 10:34–35.)

Peter had been of the opinion that only Jews were in the favor of the Lord and that Gentiles were not as acceptable. Before he had even met Cornelius, though, a vision was shown him, and he saw plainly that God was not partial. No nation or people or individual could expect to be favored above another.

From those passages of scripture we learn these basic principles:

First, all people on earth are of one blood—we stem from common ancestors, Adam and Eve.

Second, God, our Father, in his omniscient wisdom, determined premortally the nation in which we were to live.

Third, nationalities are apparently circumscribed in relation to the House of Israel.

Fourth, our Father does not favor one people over another, but accepts all those of every nation who fear him and work righteousness.

The Church, being the kingdom of God on earth, has a mission to all nations. The Lord told his disciples, "Go ye therefore, and teach all nations, baptizing them in the name of the Father, and of the Son, and of the Holy Ghost: teaching them to observe all things whatsoever I have commanded you." (Matt. 28:19–20.) These words from the lips of the Master know no national boundaries; they are not limited to any race or culture. One nation is not favored above another. The admonition is clear: "teach *all* nations."

President Spencer W. Kimball renewed this great challenge to the leaders of the Church in an address to Regional Representatives in 1974 when he said:

> The scriptures are replete with commands and promises and calls and rewards for teaching the gospel. I use the word *command* deliberately for it seems to be an insistent directive from which we, singly and collectively, cannot escape.
>
> I ask you, what did he mean when the Lord took his Twelve Apostles to the top of the Mount of Olives and said: "And ye shall be witnesses unto me both in Jerusalem, and in all Judaea, and in Samaria, and unto the uttermost part of the earth." (Acts 1:8.)
>
> These were his last words on earth before he went to his heavenly home.
>
> What is the significance of the phrase "uttermost part of the earth"? He had already covered the area known to the apostles. Was it the people in Judea? Or those in Samaria? Or the few millions in the Near East? Where were the "uttermost parts of the earth"? Did he mean the millions in what is now America? Did he include the hundreds of thousands, or even millions, in Greece, Italy, and around the Mediterranean, the

inhabitants of Central Europe? What did he mean? Or did he mean all the living people of all the world and those spirits assigned to this world to come in centuries ahead? Have we underestimated his language or its meaning? How can we be satisfied with 100,000 converts out of four billion people in the world who need the gospel?

After his crucifixion the eleven apostles assembled on a mountain in Galilee and the Savior came to them and said:

"All power is given unto me in heaven and in earth.

"Go ye therefore, and teach all nations, baptizing them in the name of the Father, and of the Son, and of the Holy Ghost:

"Teaching them to observe all things whatsoever I have commanded you: and, lo, I am with you alway, even unto the end of the world. Amen." (Matt. 28:18–20.) . . .

Again as Mark records the events after the resurrection, he upbraided those who had some doubts about his resurrection, then commanded them:

"Go ye into all the world, and preach the gospel to every creature." (Mark 16:15.) . . .

And Luke records the event—

"That repentance and remission of sins should be preached . . . among all nations, beginning at Jerusalem." (Luke 24:47.)

Again, [the Lord's] last command. Surely there is significance in these words! There was a universal need and there must be universal coverage.

As I remember the world as Moses saw it—it was a big world.

"And Moses beheld the world and the ends thereof, and all the children of men which are, and which were created." (Moses 1:8.)

I am constrained to believe that at that time the Lord knew the bounds of the habitations of man and the areas that would be settled and already knew his people who would possess this world. ("When the World Will Be Converted," *Ensign*, October 1974, 4–5.)

Several developments have taken place in recent years that significantly assist in accomplishing the commission to teach all nations. One such development that has been revealed is the building up of the Quorums of the Seventy. One of the

71

revelations formulating the constitution for the affairs of the kingdom makes this provision:

"The Twelve are a Traveling Presiding High Council, to officiate in the name of the Lord, under the direction of the Presidency of the Church, agreeable to the institution of heaven; to build up the church, and regulate all the affairs of the same in all nations." The revelation then continues to define the duties of the Seventy: "The Seventy are to act in the name of the Lord, under the direction of the Twelve or the traveling high council, in building up the church and regulating all the affairs of the same in all nations. . . . It is the duty of the traveling high council to call upon the Seventy, when they need assistance." (D&C 107:33–34, 38.)

With the rapid growth of the Church and the heavy demands on the Twelve to provide leadership and administration and teach all nations, it becomes clear why the Lord has directed the building up of the Seventy. An interesting historical parallel is recorded by Luke in the Acts of the Apostles. The foreign or Hellenistic Jews in Jerusalem were complaining that their widows were being neglected and not taken care of as well as the widows of the native Jews. When the apostles heard of this murmuring, a significant thing happened:

"Then the twelve called the multitude of the disciples unto them, and said, It is not reason that we should leave the word of God, and serve tables. Wherefore, brethren, look ye out among you seven men of honest report, full of the Holy Ghost and wisdom, whom we may appoint over this business. But we will give ourselves continually to prayer, and to the ministry of the word." (Acts 6:2–4.)

In other words, the Twelve told the disciples that it was not reasonable for them to leave their important office of teaching the gospel in order to provide for the daily welfare of the widows and serve their tables. There were other good men who could look after these duties so that the Twelve could continue to devote themselves to the charge of teaching the gospel to all persons. The result of the decision to call others to assist with the details was this:

"And the word of God increased; and the number of the disciples multiplied in Jerusalem greatly; and a great company of the priests were obedient to the faith." (Acts 6:7.)

In the brief statement of that episode, we learn these facts:

First, the Twelve determined they were not to "serve tables," or, in other words, they were not to occupy their time in the details of administration.

Second, they appointed seven men, "full of the Holy Ghost and wisdom," to look after the day-to-day needs.

Third, the Twelve then devoted their energies to the "ministry of the word."

Fourth, the word of God increased, and the gospel was carried to greater numbers.

In December 1978, the First Presidency and the Quorum of the Twelve made a similar determination that it was no longer advisable for the Twelve to occupy their time in the details of administration of the many Church departments. They delegated seven men, designated as the presidents of the First Quorum of the Seventy, to give supervision to these details so that the Twelve could devote their full energies to the overall direction of the work, and, as directed by the Doctrine and Covenants, "to build up the church, and regulate all the affairs of the same in all nations." (D&C 107:33.)

I fully believe that in the near future we will see some of the greatest advancements in spreading the gospel to all nations that have ever taken place in this dispensation or any previous dispensation. I am sure that we will be able to look back in retrospect—as a result of the decision made—and record as Luke did, "And the word of God increased." (Acts 6:7.)

Another significant development was the revelation on extending priesthood blessings to all worthy male members, regardless of race or color, which assists in accomplishing the commission to teach all nations.

From these revelations and developments, it should be

manifestly evident to members of the Church that our Father loves all of his children.

He desires all of them to embrace the gospel and come unto him. Only those who obey him and keep his commandments are favored. As members of the Lord's church, we need to lift our vision beyond personal prejudices. We need to discover the supreme truth that indeed our Father is no respecter of persons. Sometimes we unduly offend brothers and sisters of other nations by assigning exclusiveness to one nationality of people over another.

Let me cite, as an example of exclusiveness, the conflicts in recent years between the Arabs and the Jews. We do not need to apologize nor mitigate any of the prophecies concerning the Holy Land. We believe them and declare them to be true. But this does not give us justification to dogmatically pronounce that others of our Father's children are not children of promise.

We have members of the Church in the Muslim world. These are wonderful Saints, good members of the Church. They live in Iran, Egypt, Lebanon, Saudi Arabia, and other countries. Sometimes they are offended by members of the Church who give the impression that we favor only the aims of the Jews. The Church has an interest in all of Abraham's descendants, and we should remember that the history of the Arabs goes back to Abraham through his son Ishmael.

Imagine a father with many sons, each having different temperaments, aptitudes, and spiritual traits. Does he love one son less than another? Perhaps the son who is least spiritually inclined has the father's attention, prayers, and pleadings more than the others. Does that mean he loves the others less? Do you imagine our Heavenly Father loving one nationality of his offspring more exclusively than others? As members of the Church, we need to be reminded of Nephi's challenging question: "Know ye not that there are more nations than one?" (2 Ne. 29:7.)

A cabinet minister of Egypt once told me that if a bridge is ever built between Christianity and Islam, it must be built by the Mormon Church. In making inquiry as to the reason for his statement, I was impressed by his recitation of the similarities and the common bonds of brotherhood.

Both the Jews and the Arabs are children of our Father. They are both children of promise, and as a church we do not take sides. We have love for and an interest in each. The purpose of the gospel of Jesus Christ is to bring about love, unity, and brotherhood of the highest order. Like Nephi of old, may we be able to say, "I have charity for the Jew. . . . I also have charity for the Gentiles." (2 Ne. 33:8–9.)

To our friends of Judah, we say: We are your brethren of the house of Joseph—we feel a close relationship to you. We are messengers of the true covenant and bear a message that God has spoken in this day and time.

To our kinsmen of Abraham, we say: We are your brethren—we look upon no nation or nationality as second-class citizens. We invite all peoples to investigate our message and to receive our fellowship.

To our brothers and sisters of all nationalities: We bear solemn witness and testify that God has spoken in our day and time, that heavenly messengers have been sent, that God has revealed his mind and will to a prophet, Joseph Smith. And, as Andrew beckoned his brother, Simon Peter, to come and hear the Messiah, we say to one and all: "Come and see." (See John 1:35–42.)

As our Father loves all his children, we must love all people—of every race, culture, and nationality—and teach them the principles of the gospel so that they might embrace it and come to a knowledge of the divinity of the Savior. Only they are favored who keep his commandments.

I know that God is our eternal Heavenly Father, and that his son, Jesus Christ, is the Savior of the world. We will receive blessings and find exaltation by following him, keeping his commandments, and having love for and teaching all nations.

Chapter 14

THE GOLDEN
THREAD OF CHOICE

*We are given the knowledge, the help, the
enticement, and the freedom to choose the path
of eternal safety and salvation.*

Abraham Lincoln once asked, "What constitutes the bulwark
of our own liberty and independence?" He then answered, "It is
not our frowning battlements, our bristling sea coasts, our army
and our navy. . . . Our reliance is in the love of liberty which God
has planted in us." (Speech at Edwardsville, Illinois, September
11, 1858.)

There are, of course, those who, in bitterness and disbelief,
have rejected the idea of an independent spirit in man that is
capable of free will and choice and true liberty.

We declare a bright and glorious view of God and man to all
who will hear, a view revealed in and illuminated by the restored
light of the gospel of Jesus Christ. We testify of God's loving
goodness and of his eternal respect for each of us, for us as individual children of God and for what each of us may become.

"The Church of Jesus Christ of Latter-day Saints proclaims
that life is eternal, that it has purpose," President Ezra Taft
Benson declared. God has a plan "for the benefit and blessing of
us, His children. . . . Basic to [that] all-important plan is our free
agency. . . . The right of choice . . . runs like a golden thread

throughout the gospel . . . for the blessing of His children." (*The Teachings of Ezra Taft Benson* [Salt Lake City: Bookcraft, 1988], 80–81.)

Part of our reassurance about the free, noble, and progressing spirit of man comes from the glorious realization that we all existed and had our identities, and our agency, long before we came to this world. To some that will be a new thought, but the Bible teaches clearly just such an eternal view of life, a life stretching back before this world was and stretching forward into the eternities ahead.

God said to Jeremiah, "Before I formed thee in the belly I knew thee; and before thou camest forth out of the womb I sanctified thee, and I ordained thee a prophet unto the nations." (Jer. 1:5.) At another time God reminded Job that "all the sons of God shouted for joy" before there was yet any man or woman on the earth God was creating. (Job 38:7.) The Apostle Paul taught that God the Father chose us "before the foundation of the world." (Eph. 1:4.)

Where and when did all of this happen? Well, it happened long before man's mortal birth. It happened in a great premortal existence in which we developed our identities and increased our spiritual capabilities by exercising our agency and making important choices. We developed our intelligence and learned to love the truth, and we prepared to come to earth to continue our progress.

Our Father in Heaven wanted our growth to continue in mortality and to be enhanced by our freedom to choose and learn. He also wanted us to exercise our faith and our will, especially with a new physical body to master and control. But we know from both ancient and modern revelation that Satan wished to deny us our independence and agency in that now-forgotten moment long ago, even as he wishes to deny them this very hour. Indeed, Satan violently opposed the freedom of choice offered by the Father, so violently that John in the Revelation described "war in heaven" over the matter. (Rev. 12:7.) Satan would have coerced us, and he would have robbed us of that most precious of gifts if he could: our freedom to choose a divine future and the exaltation we all hope to obtain.

Through Christ and his valiant defense of our Father's plan, the course of agency and eternal aspirations prevailed. In that crucial, premortal setting, a major milestone was passed, a monumental victory was won. As a result, we would be allowed to continue to pursue what President David O. McKay once described as "an eternal principle of progress." Later Christ himself would come to earth, President McKay noted, "to perfect society by perfecting the individual, and only by the exercising of Free Agency can the individual even approach perfection." (Conference Report, April 1940, 118.)

So we came to our mortality, like Jeremiah, known by God as his literal spirit children, having the privilege to choose our personal path on matters of belief and religious conviction. With Christ's triumph in heaven in overcoming Lucifer, and later his triumph on earth in overcoming the effects of Adam's fall and the death of all mankind, "the children of men" continue "free forever, knowing good from evil; to act for themselves and not be acted upon. . . . Wherefore, men are free . . . to choose liberty and eternal life, through [Christ] the great Mediator of all men, or to choose captivity and death, according to the captivity and power of the devil; for he seeketh that all men might be miserable like unto himself." (2 Ne. 2:26–27.)

To fully understand this gift of agency and its inestimable worth, it is imperative that we understand that God's chief way of acting is by persuasion and patience and long-suffering, not by coercion and stark confrontation. He acts by gentle solicitation and by sweet enticement. He always acts with unfailing respect for the freedom and independence that we possess. He wants to help us and pleads for the chance to assist us, but he will not do so in violation of our agency. He loves us too much to do that, and doing so would run counter to his divine character.

Brigham Young once said, "That volition of [man] is free; this is a law of their existence, and the Lord cannot violate his own law; were he to do that, he would cease to be God. . . . This is a law which has always existed from all eternity, and will continue to exist throughout all the eternities to come. Every intelligent being must have the power of choice." (*Journal of Discourses* 11:272.)

To countermand and ultimately forbid our choices was Satan's way, not God's; the Father of us all simply never will do that. He will, however, stand by us forever to help us see the right path, find the right choice, respond to the true voice, and feel the influence of his undeniable Spirit. His gentle, peaceful, powerful persuasion to do right and find joy will be with us "so long as time shall last, or the earth shall stand, or there shall be one man upon the face thereof to be saved." (Moro. 7:36.)

Given the freedom to choose, we may, in fact, make wrong choices, bad choices, hurtful choices. And sometimes we do just that, but that is where the mission and the mercy of Jesus Christ come into full force and glory. He has taken upon himself the burden of all the world's risk. He has provided a mediating atonement for the wrong choices we make. He is our advocate with the Father and has paid, in advance, for the faults and foolishness we often see in the exercise of our freedom. We must accept his gift, repent of those mistakes, and follow his commandments in order to take full advantage of this redemption. The offer is always there; the way is always open. We can always, even in our darkest hour and most disastrous errors, look to the Son of God and live.

When the children of Israel returned from Egypt and stood on the threshold of the promised land, they faced the clear choice of what was before them. Of the future that was about to be theirs, the Lord said to them: "Behold, I set before you this day a blessing and a curse; a blessing, if ye obey the commandments of the Lord your God, which I command you this day: and a curse, if ye will not obey the commandments of the Lord your God." (Deut. 11:26–28.)

That is the choice the Lord puts before us as we face our own promised lands and our own bright futures. We are given the knowledge, the help, the enticement, and the freedom to choose the path of eternal safety and salvation. The choice to do so is ours. By divine decree before this world was, the actual choice is and always has been our own.

Let us be conscious of the fact that our future is being fashioned by the decisions we make. May we exercise our faith and our agency in choosing the blessings God has set before us in the great gospel plan of our Savior.

Chapter 15

"MAKE US THY TRUE UNDERSHEPHERDS"

*Like the Good Shepherd, we can help those
who have lost their way in the wilderness.*

The December 1986 message of the First Presidency to the membership of the Church included a significant invitation that read in part:

"To those who have ceased activity and to those who have become critical, we say, 'Come back. Come back and feast at the table of the Lord, and taste again the sweet and satisfying fruits of fellowship with the Saints.' We are confident that many have longed to return, but have felt awkward about doing so. We assure you that you will find open arms to receive you and willing hands to assist you." (*Ensign*, March 1986, 88.)

I think all of us were impressed by this magnanimous appeal, which is akin to what the prophet Alma stated in the Book of Mormon regarding an invitation that was extended by the Lord:

"Behold, he sendeth an invitation unto all men, for the arms of mercy are extended towards them, and he saith: Repent, and I will receive you. Yea, he saith: Come unto me and ye shall partake of the fruit of the tree of life; yea, ye shall eat and drink of the bread and the waters of life freely; yea, come unto me and bring forth works of righteousness." (Alma 5:33–35.)

Each of us should read and reread the parable of the lost sheep found in the New Testament:

"What man of you, having an hundred sheep, if he lose one of them, doth not leave the ninety and nine in the wilderness, and go after that which is lost, until he find it? And when he hath found it, he layeth it on his shoulders, rejoicing. And when he cometh home, he calleth together his friends and neighbours, saying unto them, Rejoice with me; for I have found my sheep which was lost.

"I say unto you, that likewise joy shall be in heaven over one sinner that repenteth, more than over ninety and nine just persons, which need no repentance." (Luke 15:4–7.)

The Prophet Joseph Smith significantly altered one verse of this account in the Joseph Smith Translation. It reads: "What man of you, having an hundred sheep, if he lose one of them, doth not leave the ninety and nine, *and go into the wilderness after that which is lost,* until he find it?" (JST Luke 15:4; italics added.)

That translation suggests that the shepherd should leave his secure flock and go out into the wilderness—that is, go out into the world after that which is lost. Lost from what? Lost from the flock where there is protection and security. I hope the message of that parable will be impressed on each man who has priesthood responsibility.

When President Benson was president of the Quorum of the Twelve, he made a great appeal to priesthood leaders in an address titled "A Call to the Priesthood: 'Feed My Sheep.'" I think it would be well for us to reread his message. It should be reviewed frequently by every priesthood leader. In this address, President Benson asked:

> *Shepherds—stake presidents, bishops, quorum leaders:*
> Do you leave the ninety and nine and search after the lost one?
> Do you call and appoint advisers and others who can reach impressionable youth and visit them on their "own ground"?
> Have you fully implemented the youth program, and are you using this program to meet the individual needs of the youth?

Are you watchful over the young singles, the divorced, and those with special needs?

Do you carefully and spiritually prepare those who enter military service?

Are you especially attentive to young men between the transition period from Aaronic Priesthood to Melchizedek Priesthood?

Bishops, do you make sure they come under the care of their new shepherd, the quorum president?

Do you provide significant Church-service opportunities for our returned missionaries so these young men and women do not drift into inactivity because they do not have occasion to serve as they have been doing . . . ?

Do you use visiting teachers to augment home teaching?

Are you teaching fathers their duties?

Do you have temple preparation seminars to encourage prospective elders to prepare for the Melchizedek Priesthood and the temple?

Do you have older prospective elders assigned to the high priests and invited to join those with whom they would feel most comfortable?

Are younger prospective elders invited to participate with the elders quorums?

Some leaders say that some men are past hope, but, as the angel told Abraham, nothing is impossible with the Lord! (See Gen. 18:14.) One brother who was regarded by some as a hopeless case tearfully exclaimed to the temple worker at the sealing altar, "I don't know why I waited so long for this blessing!"

In a recent Saturday evening meeting of leaders I heard a determined brother state, "I've sure had a time with the devil since I started to become active. Prior to that time, I just went along with him."

Are we helping the one who needs help because he has started on the way back to full activity? (*Ensign*, May 1983, 45.)

A study of those questions will give a priesthood leader an agenda for activation possibilities in every ward and stake in Zion.

Over the years the Church has made some monumental efforts to recover those who are less active because of their pre-occupation with the world, neglect by Church leaders, and will-ful rebellion. Some of those efforts have been designated with names such as "project temple," "Senior Aaronic program," "temple seminar," and "activation programs." And all to what end? It is to save the souls of our brothers and sisters and see that they have the ordinances of exaltation.

While I was serving as a stake president in the Los Angeles area, my counselors and I asked our bishops to carefully select four or five couples who wanted to further their progress in the Church. Some were less active, others new converts, but they were motivated to spiritually progress. We got them together in a stake class and taught them the gospel. Rather than emphasiz-ing the temple, we stressed a better relationship with our Heavenly Father and his Son, Jesus Christ. Our careful selection process assured success, and the majority of these couples did become active and go to the temple.

Let me share an experience or two. We had a brother in one of the wards who didn't attend any meetings. His wife was not a member. She was somewhat hostile, so we could not send home teachers to the home. The bishop approached this brother by telling him that the brother had a relationship with the Savior he needed to expand and enlarge. The brother explained to the bishop the problem with his nonmember wife, so the bishop talked to her, emphasizing the same approach—a relationship with the Lord that needed to be expanded. She still was not receptive but was happy to learn that Latter-day Saints believed in Christ, and consequently, she dropped some of her defenses.

Success did not come immediately, but those who visited the home kept stressing the couple's relationship with the Lord. In time she became friendly, and finally she consented to come with her husband to the stake class taught by members of the high council. We stressed the covenant one makes at baptism and other covenants. Eventually she became a member of the Church and he became a productive priesthood leader. Today all of their family members are active in the Church.

I am impressed by a statement on the title page of the Book of Mormon that describes one of the purposes of that sacred book: "That they [the House of Israel in the latter days] may know the covenants of the Lord." That was the emphasis we as a stake presidency felt impressed to make to those less active. We tried to appeal to them on the basis of the importance of the covenants they had made with the Lord; then we taught them the importance of the covenant of baptism and additional covenants they could make that would unite them as an eternal family.

Another example. My ward bishop assigned me as a ward teacher (home teaching was ward teaching in those days) to a brother who boasted he was the oldest deacon in the Church. His problem was that he loved to play golf on Sunday. It was discouraging to meet month after month with him and his wife and see no apparent progress. But finally, the right word was said to him and it struck a responsive chord. The word was *covenant.* We asked him, "What does the covenant of baptism mean to you?" His expression changed, and for the first time we saw a serious side to him. Eventually he came to our classes, gave up golf, and took his wife to the temple. He is now deceased, but she is very active as a temple worker.

Now the question: What should we do to help those who have lost their way in the wilderness?

Because of what the Master said about leaving the ninety-nine and going into the wilderness to seek the one that is lost, and because of the invitation of the First Presidency to those who have ceased activity or have been critical to "come back," we invite you to become involved in saving souls. Reach out to the less active and realize the joy that will come to you and those you help if you and they will take part in extending invitations to come back and feast at the table of the Lord.

The Lord, our Good Shepherd, expects us to be his undershepherds and recover those who are struggling or are lost. We can't tell you how to do it, but as you become involved and seek inspiration, success will result from efforts in your areas, regions, stakes, and wards. Some stakes have responded to previous pleadings and have had remarkable success.

The words of a familiar hymn contain the Savior's appeal to us:

> *Hark! he is earnestly calling,*
> *Tenderly pleading today:*
> *"Will you not seek for my lost ones,*
> *Off from my shelter astray?"*

And that hymn, sung often, indicates what our response should be:

> *Make us thy true undershepherds;*
> *Give us a love that is deep.*
> *Send us out into the desert,*
> *Seeking thy wandering sheep.*
> —Hymns, *no. 221*

If we do this, eternal blessings will come to us.

Part 3

FACING TRIALS
AND TRIBULATIONS

*"In the world ye shall have tribulation: but be
of good cheer; I have overcome the world."*
(John 16:33)

Chapter 16

AN ANCHOR TO
THE SOULS OF MEN

*We will have our difficulties the way every
generation has had difficulties. But with the
gospel of Jesus Christ, we have hope,
promise, and reassurance.*

Life has a fair number of challenges in it, and that's true of
life in the 1990s. Indeed, you may be feeling that you have more
than your share of problems. These concerns may be global difficulties, such as the devastating famine we see in Africa and other
places in the world, or the incessant sounds of war in the former
Yugoslavia, or the Middle East, or India, or Ireland, or so many
other locations round the world. Unfortunately, some of these
wars have religious or ethnic overtones, and that makes them
even more tragic, if that is possible.

These past few years, we have seen our fair share of economic difficulties and recession in every nation. Sometimes those
economic challenges get translated into very immediate problems for college students and those trying to earn a living, and
perhaps start a family, in their early adult years.

Years ago there was a popular music group formed at
Brigham Young University named the Three D's. They took that
name from their three singers' first names. My fear is that if in the
nineties our young people were to form a popular singing group,

they might still call themselves the Three D's, but that could be for Despair, Doom, and Discouragement.

Despair, Doom, and Discouragement are not acceptable views of life for a Latter-day Saint. However high on the charts they are on the hit parade of contemporary news, we must not walk on our lower lip every time a few difficult moments happen to confront us.

I am just a couple of years older than most of you, and in those few extra months I have seen a bit more of life than you have. I want you to know that there have always been some difficulties in mortal life, and there always will be. But knowing what we know, and living as we are supposed to live, there really is no place, no excuse, for pessimism and despair.

In my lifetime I have seen two world wars, plus Korea, plus Vietnam and all that you are currently witnessing. I have worked my way through the Depression and managed to go to law school while starting a young family at the same time. I have seen stock markets and world economics go crazy, and I have seen a few despots and tyrants go crazy, all of which caused quite a bit of trouble around the world in the process.

So I hope you won't believe all the world's difficulties have been wedged into your decade, or that things have never been worse than they are for you personally, or that they will never get better. I reassure you that things have been worse and they *will* always get better. They always do—especially when we live and love the gospel of Jesus Christ and give it a chance to flourish in our lives.

Here are some actual comments that have been passed on to me in recent months:

This comes from a fine returned missionary: "Why should I date and get serious with a girl? I am not sure I even want to marry and bring a family into this kind of world. I am not very sure about my own future. How can I take the responsibility for the future of others whom I would love and care about and want to be happy?"

Here's another from a high school student: "I hope I die

before all these terrible things happen that people are talking about. I don't want to be on the earth when there is so much trouble."

This from a recent college graduate: "I am doing the best I can, but I wonder if there is much reason to even plan for the future, let alone retirement. The world probably won't last that long anyway."

Well, my, my, my. Isn't that a fine view of things? Sounds like we all ought to go eat a big plate of worms.

Contrary to what some might say, you have every reason in this world to be happy and to be optimistic and to be confident. Every generation since time began has had some things to overcome and some problems to work out. Furthermore, every individual person has a particular set of challenges that sometimes seem to be earmarked for us personally. We understood that in our premortal existence.

Prophets and apostles of the Church have faced some of those personal difficulties. I acknowledge that I have faced a few, and you will undoubtedly face some of your own now and later in your life. When these experiences humble us and refine us and teach us and bless us, they can be powerful instruments in the hands of God to make us better people, to make us more grateful, more loving, and more considerate of other people in their own times of difficulty.

Yes, we all have difficult moments, individually and collectively, but even in the most severe of times, anciently or in modern times, those problems and prophecies were never intended to do anything but bless the righteous and help those who are less righteous move toward repentance. God loves us, and the scriptures tell us he "gave his only begotten Son, that whosoever believeth in him should not perish, but have everlasting life. For God sent not his Son into the world to condemn the world; but that the world through him might be saved." (John 3:16–17.)

The scriptures also indicate that there will be seasons of time when the whole world will have some difficulty. We know that in our dispensation, unrighteousness will, unfortunately, be quite

91

evident, and it will bring its inevitable difficulties and pain and punishment. God will cut short that unrighteousness in his own due time, but our task is to live fully and faithfully and not worry ourselves sick about the woes of the world or when it will end. Our task is to have the gospel in our lives and to be a bright light, a city set on the hill, that reflects the beauty of the gospel of Jesus Christ and the joy and happiness that will always come to every people in every age who keep the commandments.

In this last dispensation there will be great tribulation. We know that there will be wars and rumors of wars and that the whole earth will be in commotion. All dispensations have had their perilous times, but our day will include genuine peril. Evil men will flourish, but then evil men have very often flourished. Calamities will come and iniquity will abound. (See Matt. 24:21; D&C 45:26–27; 2 Tim. 3:1, 13.)

Inevitably the natural result of some of these kinds of prophecies is fear, and that is not fear limited to a younger generation. It is fear shared by those of any age who don't understand what we understand.

But I want to stress that these feelings are not necessary for faithful Latter-day Saints, and they do not come from God. To ancient Israel, the great Jehovah said: "Be strong and of a good courage, fear not, nor be afraid of them: for the Lord thy God, he it is that doth go with thee; he will not fail thee, nor forsake thee. . . . And the Lord, he it is that doth go before thee; he will be with thee, he will not fail thee, neither forsake thee: fear not, neither be dismayed." (Deut. 31:6, 8.)

And to the Saints in modern Israel, the Lord has given this wonderful reassurance: "Fear not, little children, for you are mine, and I have overcome the world, and you are of them that my Father hath given me." (D&C 50:41.) "Verily I say unto you my friends, fear not, let your hearts be comforted; yea, rejoice evermore, and in everything give thanks." (D&C 98:1.)

In light of such counsel, I think it is incumbent upon us to rejoice a little more and despair a little less, to give thanks for what we have and for the magnitude of God's blessings to us, and to talk a little less about what we may not have or what anxiety may accompany difficult times in this or any generation.

For Latter-day Saints this is a time of great hope and excitement—one of the greatest eras in the Restoration and therefore one of the greatest eras in any dispensation, inasmuch as ours is the greatest of all dispensations. We need to have faith and hope, two of the great fundamental virtues of any discipleship of Christ. We must continue to exercise confidence in God, inasmuch as that is the first principle in our code of belief. We must believe that God has all power, that he loves us, and that his work will not be stopped or frustrated in our individual lives or in the world generally. He will bless us as a people because he always has blessed us as a people. He will bless us as individuals because he always has blessed us as individuals.

Listen to this marvelous counsel given by President Joseph F. Smith nearly ninety years ago. It sounds as if people in that day might have been a little anxious about their future as well. I quote:

"You do not need to worry in the least, the Lord will take care of you and bless you. He will also take care of His servants, and will bless them and help them to accomplish His purposes; and all the powers of darkness combined in earth and in hell cannot prevent it. . . . He has stretched forth His hand to accomplish his purposes, and the arm of flesh cannot stay it. He will cut His work short in righteousness, and will hasten His purposes in His own time. It is only necessary for us to try with our might to keep pace with the onward progress of the work of the Lord, then God will preserve and protect us, and will prepare the way before us, that we shall live and multiply and replenish the earth and always do His will." (Conference Report, October 1905, 5–6.)

More recently, Elder Marion G. Romney, then of the Quorum of the Twelve, counseled the Church in 1966, when the world also knew some difficulty. An American president had been assassinated, communism was alive and menacing, and a war was beginning to widen in Southeast Asia. My sons had some of the same anxieties young adults today have about life and marriage and the future. Here's what President Romney said then:

"Naturally, believing Christians, even those who have a mature faith in the gospel, are concerned and disturbed by the lowering clouds on the horizon. But they need not be surprised or frantic about their portent, for, as has already been said, at the very beginning of this last dispensation the Lord made it abundantly clear that through the tribulations and calamity that he foresaw and foretold and that we now see coming upon us, there would be a people who, through acceptance and obedience to the gospel, would be able to recognize and resist the powers of evil, build up the promised Zion, and prepare to meet the Christ and be with him in the blessed millennium. And we know further that it is possible for every one of us, who will, to have a place among those people. It is this assurance and this expectation that give us understanding of the Lord's admonition, 'Be not troubled.'" (Conference Report, October 1966, 53–54.)

Let me offer a third example from yet another moment of difficulty in the world. In the midst of the most devastating international conflagration the modern world has ever seen, Elder John A. Widtsoe of the Council of the Twelve counseled people who were worried. Nazism was on the march, there was war in the Pacific, and nation after nation seemed to be drawn into war. This is what Brother Widtsoe said in 1942:

"Above the roar of cannon and airplane, the maneuvers and plans of men, the Lord always determines the tide of battle. So far and no farther does He permit the evil one to go in his career to create human misery. The Lord is ever victorious; He is the Master to whose will Satan is subject. Though all hell may rage, and men may follow evil, the purposes of the Lord will not fail." (Conference Report, April 1942, p. 34.)

I promise you in the name of the Lord whose servant I am that God will always protect and care for his people. We will have our difficulties the way every generation and people have had difficulties. But with the gospel of Jesus Christ, you have every hope and promise and reassurance. The Lord has power over his Saints and will always prepare places of peace, defense, and safety for his people. When we have faith in God, we can hope for a better world—for us personally, and for all mankind. The prophet Ether taught anciently (and he knew something about troubles): "Wherefore, whoso believeth in God might with surety hope for a better world, yea, even a place at the right hand of God, which hope cometh of faith, maketh an anchor to the souls of men, which would make them sure and steadfast, always abounding in good works, being led to glorify God." (Ether 12:4.)

Disciples of Christ in every generation are invited, indeed commanded, to be filled with a perfect brightness of hope. (See 2 Ne. 31:20.)

This faith and hope of which I speak is not a Pollyanna-like approach to significant personal and public problems. I don't believe we can wake up in the morning and simply by drawing a big "happy face" on the chalkboard believe that is going to take care of the world's difficulties. But if our faith and hope are anchored in Christ, in his teachings, commandments, and promises, then we are able to count on something truly remarkable, genuinely miraculous, which can part the Red Sea and lead modern Israel to a place "where none shall come to hurt or make afraid." (Hymns, no. 30.) Fear, which can come upon people in difficult days, is a principal weapon in the arsenal Satan uses to make mankind unhappy. He who fears loses strength for the combat of life in the fight against evil. Therefore the power of the evil one always tries to generate fear in human hearts. In every age and in every era, mankind has faced fear.

As children of God and descendants of Abraham, Isaac, and Jacob, we must seek to dispel fear from among people. A timid, fearing people cannot do their work well, and they cannot do God's work at all. The Latter-day Saints have a divinely assigned mission to fulfill that simply must not be dissipated in fear and anxiety.

Elder Widtsoe said, "The key to the conquest of fear has been given through the Prophet Joseph Smith. 'If ye are prepared ye shall not fear.' (D&C 38:30.) That divine message needs repeating today in every stake and ward." (Conference Report, April 1942, 33.)

Are we prepared to surrender to God's commandments? Are we prepared to achieve victory over our appetites? Are we prepared to obey righteous law? According to Elder Widtsoe, if we can honestly answer yes to those questions, we can bid fear to depart from our lives. Surely the degree of fear in our hearts may well be measured by our preparation to live righteously—living in a way that should characterize every Latter-day Saint in every age and time.

Let me close with one of the greatest statements I have ever read from Joseph Smith, who faced such immense difficulties in his life and who, of course, paid the ultimate price for his victory. But he *was* victorious, and he was a happy, robust, optimistic man. Those who knew him felt his strength and courage, even in the darkest of times. He did not sag in spirits, or remain long in any despondency.

He said about our time that ours is the moment "upon which prophets, priests and kings [in ages past] have dwelt with peculiar delight; [all these ancient witnesses for God] have looked forward with joyful anticipation to the day in which we live; and fired with heavenly and joyful anticipations they have sung and written and prophesied of this our day; . . . we are the favored people that God has [chosen] to bring about the Latter-day glory." (*History of the Church* 4:609–10.)

What a privilege! What an honor! What a responsibility! And what joy! We have every reason in time and eternity to rejoice and give thanks for the quality of our lives and the promises we have been given.

Chapter 17

GOD WILL HAVE A TRIED PEOPLE

*The same forces of resistance which
prevent our progress afford us also
opportunities to overcome.*

A few years ago we were standing in a large crowd of people gathered early in the morning along the waterfront of Apia Harbor in Samoa. It was the occasion of the National Holidays, when hundreds of people came to watch the *fautasi*, or longboat, races that sweep in from the ocean to the calmer waters of the harbor to cross the finish line.

The crowd was restless, and most eyes were turned toward the sea, watching for the first glimpse of the *fautasis*. Suddenly there was a roar from the crowd as the boats came into sight in the distance. Each of them had a crew of fifty powerful oarsmen dipping and pulling the oars with a rhythm that forced the crafts through the waves and foaming water—a beautiful sight.

The boats and men were soon in full view as they raced toward the finish. Even though these powerful men pulled with their might, the weight of a boat with fifty men moved against a powerful adverse force, the resistance of the water.

The cheering of the crowd reached a crescendo when the first longboat crossed the finish line. We walked over to the place where the boats docked after the race had concluded. One of the

97

oarsmen explained to us that the prow of the *fautasi* is so constructed that it cuts through and divides the water to help overcome the resistance that retards the speed of the boat. He further explained that the pulling of the oars against the resistance of the water creates the force that causes the boat to move forward. Resistance creates both the opposition and the forward movement.

Friction, or resistance, is an interesting phenomenon. Without this force, a person or vehicle could not move about or, if already in motion, could not be stopped except by collision. Simple things like nails, screws, and bolts would not stay in place; a cork would not stay in a bottle; a light globe would drop from its socket; a lid would not stay on a jar.

The law of friction or resistance that we think of as only applying to science seems to find application in our personal lives. This is probably what Lehi was referring to when he spoke to his son Jacob. He reminded Jacob of the afflictions and sorrows that had come to him because of the rudeness of his brethren, and told him how these afflictions would ultimately result in good. These are the words of Jacob to his son: "Thou knowest the greatness of God; and he shall consecrate thine afflictions for thy gain." (2 Ne. 2:2.)

In other words, the afflictions that had come to Jacob in the form of opposition or resistance would be for his good. Then Lehi added these words that have become classic: "For it must needs be, that there is an opposition in all things. If not so, . . . righteousness could not be brought to pass, neither wickedness, neither holiness nor misery, neither good nor bad." (2 Ne. 2:11.)

We came to mortal life to encounter resistance. It was part of the plan for our eternal progress. Without temptation, sickness, pain, and sorrow, there could be no goodness, virtue, appreciation for well-being, or joy. The law of opposition makes freedom of choice possible; therefore, our Heavenly Father has commanded his children, "Choose ye this day, to serve the Lord God who made you." (Moses 6:33.) He has counseled us to yield to his spirit and resist temptation. Free agency, of course, permits us to oppose his directions; thus, we see many who resist the truth and yield to temptation.

Today the Church stands at the summit of over a century and a half of progress. The terrain over which we have traveled is a grim reminder that struggle, persecution, and sorrow have been the lot of our forebears. Kirtland, Jackson County, Clay County, Haun's Mill, and Nauvoo seem synonymous with suffering, a part of the tribulation the Lord promised that his people would have to endure. (See D&C 58:3.)

As we look back in retrospect, we see that it was because of the opposition encountered in our early history that our progress today has been made possible. Out of that cauldron of persecution and heartache, the Lord answered the soul-cry of the Prophet Joseph Smith in these words: "Thine adversity and thine afflictions shall be but a small moment; and then, if thou endure it well, God shall exalt thee on high. . . . If thou art called to pass through tribulation, . . . know thou, my son, that all these things shall give thee experience, and shall be for thy good." (D&C 121:7–8; 122:5, 7.)

By the tribulation well endured by numerous of our progenitors, a desert blossomed as a rose (see Isa. 35:1), a tried and persecuted people provided a heritage of faith, and Zion put on her beautiful garments for all to see (see D&C 82:14).

Church history provides us with a lesson that when resistance and opposition are greatest, our faith, commitment, and growth have the greatest opportunity for advancement; when opposition is least, the tendency is to be complacent and lose faith. President Brigham Young said, "Let any people enjoy peace and quietness, unmolested, undisturbed,—never be persecuted for their religion, and they are very likely to neglect their duty, to become cold and indifferent, and lose their faith." (*Journal of Discourses* 7:42.) This lesson, which applies to the Church collectively, also applies to individuals.

Documented in scripture are episodes from the lives of many former-day Saints who, by personal sacrifice, opposition, and adversity, achieved their exaltation. From their biographies of struggle, I offer their testaments of faithful endurance.

The classic example of faithful endurance was the Old Testament prophet Job. He lost all his possessions, he suffered great personal affliction and physical pain, some of his children met tragic death, and even his friends deserted him. Yet he proclaimed his faith: "[God] knoweth the way that I take: when he hath tried me, I shall come forth as gold. . . . His way have I kept, and not declined." (Job 23:10–11.)

We turn the pages to another exemplar of faith, father Abraham. He fought in time of war, went through a period of extensive famine, saw his own father turn away from the priesthood, and suffered persecution for his faith, almost to the point of his own death. After years of waiting for a son, he was ordered to sacrifice him to the Lord. He also experienced the sorrow of the loss of his beloved wife Sarah.

To the early Saints of this dispensation, the Lord said, "I, the Lord, have suffered the affliction to come upon them. . . . They must needs be chastened and tried, even as Abraham." (D&C 101:2, 4.)

Abraham's grandson Jacob was also no stranger to adversity. He was estranged from his twin brother as a young man and didn't return home to see his father, mother, or brother for many years. He lived a life of mourning for a favorite son, whom he thought dead, but who had been sold into slavery. He buried his beloved Rachel after she gave birth to his last-born son, Benjamin. He knew the personal sorrow of sons who were not valiant, but still he blessed their days and posterity so that their descendants are honored to be called the House of Jacob, the House of Israel.

The New Testament records the life of Paul of Tarsus. From the day of his dramatic conversion, he experienced great trial and personal affliction. He was imprisoned for his faith, beaten, stoned, and, in his own words, buffeted by Satan. Yet he wrote: "Most gladly . . . will I . . . glory in my infirmities, that the power of Christ may rest upon me." (2 Cor. 12:9.) Comparing his own

100

adversity to that of Paul, the Prophet Joseph once wrote, "I feel, like Paul, to glory in tribulation; for to this day has the God of my fathers delivered me." (D&C 127:2.)

Last, I refer to the life of Nephi from the Book of Mormon as an example of faithful endurance. With his parents, he left prosperous circumstances in Jerusalem and for eight years, in great affliction, journeyed in the wilderness. The family then crossed uncharted seas to a new land. During this period, Nephi was assailed, ridiculed, and persecuted by members of his household. Following the death of his father, Nephi and other family members had to separate themselves from his older brothers because they sought his life. Out of his despair, he declared, "My God hath been my support; he hath led me through mine afflictions in the wilderness; and he hath preserved me upon the waters of the great deep." (2 Ne. 4:20.)

These are biographies of faith—men whom God has honored because they relied on him in times of their extremity. They learned the truth that God chose them "in the furnace of affliction." (Isa. 48:10.)

Today other biographies of faith are being written—Saints who, like Job, suffer physical pain, emotional sorrow, and even disloyalty from friends, yet remain faithful; Saints who, like Jacob, see sons and daughters not so valiant as they should be, but who bless them for their potential, Saints who, like Paul, endure great ridicule but endure to the end; Saints who, like Nephi, must separate themselves from family because of their commitment to the gospel. There are those who know pain and sorrow because of loss of loved ones; who know spiritual sorrow because children go astray; who experience loss of health, financial reverses, and emotional distress, and yet, like Job, resolve, "When he hath tried me, I shall come forth as gold." (Job 23:10.)

President Spencer W. Kimball spoke from experience when he wrote these words: "Being human, we would expel from our lives physical pain and mental anguish and assure ourselves of continual ease and comfort, but if we were to close the doors upon sorrow and distress, we might be excluding our greatest

101

friends and benefactors. Suffering can make saints of people as they learn patience, long-suffering, and self-mastery." (*Faith Precedes the Miracle* [Salt Lake City: Deseret Book, 1972], 98.)

We stand on the summit of more than 150 years of Church history, yet there are other summits to climb before the work of God is crowned with victory. There will be tribulations collectively and hardships personally—that resistance so essential to the eternal plan.

What makes us imagine that we may be immune from the same experiences that refined the lives of former-day Saints? We must remember that the same forces of resistance that prevent our progress also afford us opportunities to overcome. God will have a tried people!

May God bless us to endure well the purpose for which we were sent.

Chapter 18

WHAT IS
TRUE GREATNESS?

*True greatness is to do one's best in the face of
the commonplace struggles of life—and to
continue to endure and to persevere in the
ongoing difficulties of life.*

Many Latter-day Saints are happy and enjoying the opportunities life offers. Yet I am concerned that some among us are unhappy. Some of us feel that we are falling short of our expected ideals. I have particular concern for those who have lived righteously but think, because they haven't achieved in the world or in the Church what others have achieved, that they have failed. Each of us desires to achieve a measure of greatness in this life. And why shouldn't we? As someone once noted, there is within each of us a giant struggling with celestial homesickness. (See Heb. 11:13–16; D&C 45:11–14.)

Realizing who we are and what we may become assures us that with God nothing is really impossible. From the time we learn that Jesus wants us for a Sunbeam through the time we learn more fully the basic principles of the gospel, we are taught to strive for perfection. It is not new to us, then, to talk of the importance of achievement. The difficulty arises when inflated expectations of the world alter the definition of greatness.

What is true greatness? What is it that makes a person great?

We live in a world that seems to worship its own kind of greatness and to produce its own kind of heroes. In recent years surveys of young people ages eighteen through twenty-four have revealed that today's youth prefer the "strong, go-it-alone, conquer-against-all-odds" individuals and that they clearly seek to pattern their lives after the glamorous and "boundlessly rich." During the 1950s, heroes included Winston Churchill, Albert Schweitzer, President Harry Truman, Queen Elizabeth, and Helen Keller, the blind and deaf writer-lecturer. These were figures who either helped shape history or were noted for their inspiring lives. Today, many of the top ten heroes are movie stars and other entertainers, which suggests something of a shift in our attitudes.

It's true that most of the world's heroes don't last very long in the public mind; magazines, billboards, and television commercials bombard us with pictures of individuals with perfect teeth and flawless features, wearing stylish clothes and doing whatever it is that "successful" people do. Nevertheless, there is no lack of champions and great achievers. We hear almost daily of athletes breaking records; scientists inventing marvelous new devices, machines, and processes; and doctors saving lives in new ways. We also hear of exceptionally gifted musicians and entertainers and of unusually talented artists, architects, and builders.

Because we are being constantly exposed to the world's definition of *greatness*, it is understandable that we might make comparisons between what we are and what others are—or seem to be—and also between what we have and what others have. Although it is true that making comparisons can be beneficial and may motivate us to accomplish much good and to improve our lives, we often allow unfair and improper comparisons to destroy our happiness when they cause us to feel unfulfilled or inadequate or unsuccessful. Sometimes, because of these feelings, we are led into error and dwell on our failures while ignoring aspects of our lives that may contain elements of true greatness.

In 1905, President Joseph F. Smith made this most profound statement about true greatness: "Those things which we call extraordinary, remarkable, or unusual may make history, but they do not make real life. After all, to do well those things which God ordained to be the common lot of all mankind, is the truest greatness. To be a successful father or a successful mother is greater than to be a successful general or a successful statesman." (*Juvenile Instructor*, December 15, 1905, 752.)

This statement raises a query: What are the things God has ordained to be "the common lot of all mankind"? Surely they include the things that must be done in order to be a good father or a good mother, a good son or a good daughter, a good student or a good roommate or a good neighbor.

Pablo Casals, the great cellist, spent the morning on the day he died—at the age of ninety-five—practicing scales on his cello. Giving consistent effort in the little things in day-to-day life leads to true greatness. Specifically, it is the thousands of little deeds and tasks of service and sacrifice that constitute the giving, or losing, of one's life for others and for the Lord. These things include gaining a knowledge of our Father in Heaven and the gospel, and bringing others into the faith and fellowship of his kingdom. They also do not usually receive the attention or the adulation of the world.

Joseph Smith is not generally remembered as a general, mayor, architect, editor, or presidential candidate. We remember him as the prophet of the Restoration, a man committed to the love of God and the furthering of His work. The Prophet Joseph was an everyday Christian. He was concerned about the small things, the daily tasks of service and caring for others. As a thirteen-year-old boy, Lyman O. Littlefield accompanied the camp of Zion, which marched from Ohio to Missouri. He later narrated this incident of a small yet personally significant act of service in the life of the Prophet:

"The journey was extremely toilsome for all, and the physical suffering, coupled with the knowledge of the persecutions endured by our brethren whom we were traveling to succor, caused me to lapse one day into a state of melancholy. As the camp was making ready to depart I sat tired and brooding by the roadside. The Prophet was the busiest man of the camp; and yet when he saw me, he turned from the great press of other duties to say a word of comfort to a child. Placing his hand upon my head, he said, 'Is there no place for you, my boy? If not, we must make one.' This circumstance made an impression upon my mind which long lapse of time and cares of riper years have not effaced." (In George Q. Cannon, *Life of Joseph Smith the Prophet* [Salt Lake City: Deseret Book, 1964], 344.)

On another occasion, when Governor Carlin of Illinois sent Sheriff Thomas King of Adams County and several others as a posse to apprehend the Prophet and deliver him to the emissaries of Governor Boggs of Missouri, Sheriff King became deathly ill. At Nauvoo the Prophet took the sheriff to his home and nursed him like a brother for four days. (Ibid., 373.) Small, kind, and yet significant acts of service were not occasional for the Prophet.

Writing about the opening of the store in Nauvoo, Illinois, Elder George Q. Cannon recorded: "The Prophet himself did not hesitate to engage in mercantile and industrial pursuits; the gospel which he preached was one of temporal salvation as well as spiritual exaltation; and he was willing to perform his share of the practical labor. This he did with no thought of personal gain." (Ibid., 385–86.)

And in a letter, the Prophet wrote: "The store has been filled to overflowing and I have stood behind the counter all day, distributing goods as steadily as any clerk you ever saw, to oblige those who were compelled to go without their Christmas and New Year's dinners for the want of a little sugar, molasses, raisins, etc.; and to please myself also, for I love to wait upon the Saints and to be a servant to all, hoping that I may be exalted in the due time of the Lord."

About this scene, President Cannon commented: "What a picture is presented here! A man chosen by the Lord to lay the foundation of His Church and to be its Prophet and President, takes joy and pride in waiting upon his brethren and sisters like a servant. The self-elected ministers of Christ in the world are forever jealous of their dignity and fearful of showing disrespect to their cloth; but Joseph never saw the day when he did not feel that he was serving God and obtaining favor in the sight of Jesus Christ by showing kindness and attention 'even unto the least of these.' " (Ibid., 385–86.)

To be a successful elders quorum secretary or Relief Society teacher or loving neighbor or listening friend is much of what true greatness is all about. To do one's best in the face of the commonplace struggles of life, and possibly in the face of failure, and to continue to endure and to persevere in the ongoing difficulties of life when those struggles and tasks contribute to others' progress and happiness and one's own eternal salvation—this is true greatness.

We all want to achieve a measure of greatness in this life. Many have already achieved great things; others are striving to achieve greatness. Let me encourage you to achieve and, at the same time, to remember who you are. Don't let the illusion of fleeting worldly greatness overcome you. Many people are losing their souls to such temptations. Your good name is not worth selling—for any price. True greatness is to remain true: "True to the faith that our parents have cherished,/True to the truth for which martyrs have perished." (*Hymns*, no. 254.)

I am confident that there are many great, unnoticed, and forgotten heroes among us. I am speaking of those who quietly and consistently do the things they ought to do. I am talking about those who are always there and always willing. I am referring to the uncommon valor of the mother who, hour after hour, day and night, stays with and cares for a sick child while her husband is at work or in school. I am including those who volunteer to give blood or to work with the elderly. I am thinking about those who faithfully fulfill their priesthood and church responsibilities, and of the students who write home regularly to thank their parents for their love and support.

I am also talking about those who instill in others faith and a desire to live the gospel—those who actively work to build and mold the lives of others physically, socially, and spiritually. I am referring to those who are honest and kind and hardworking in their daily tasks, but who are also servants of the Master and shepherds of his sheep.

Now, I do not mean to discount the great accomplishments of the world that have given us so many opportunities and provide culture and order and excitement in our lives. I am merely suggesting that we try to focus more clearly on the things in life that will be of greatest worth. You will remember that it was the Savior who said, "He that is greatest among you shall be your servant." (Matt. 23:11.)

Each of us has seen individuals become wealthy or successful almost instantaneously, almost overnight. But I believe that even though this kind of success may come to some without prolonged struggle, there is no such thing as instant greatness. The achievement of true greatness is a long-term process. It may involve occasional setbacks. The end result may not always be clearly visible, but it seems that it always requires regular, consistent, small, and sometimes ordinary and mundane steps over a long period of time. We should remember that it was the Lord who said, "Out of small things proceedeth that which is great." (D&C 64:33.)

True greatness is never a result of a chance occurrence or a one-time effort or achievement. Greatness requires the development of character. It requires a multitude of correct decisions in the everyday choices between good and evil that Elder Boyd K. Packer spoke about when he said, "Over the years these little choices will be bundled together and show clearly what we value." (*Ensign*, November 1980, 21.) Those choices will also show clearly what we are.

As we evaluate our lives, it is important that we look not only at our accomplishments but also at the conditions under which we have labored. We are each unique; we have each had different starting points in the race of life; we each have a unique mixture of talents and skills; we each have our own set of challenges and constraints with which to contend. Therefore, our judgment of ourselves and our achievements should not merely include the size, the magnitude, and the number of our accomplishments; it should also include the conditions that have existed and the effects that our efforts have had on others.

It is this last aspect of our self-evaluation—the effects of our lives on the lives of others—that will help us to understand why some of the common, ordinary work of life should be valued so highly. Frequently it is the commonplace tasks we perform that have the greatest positive effects on the lives of others, as compared with the things that the world so often relates to greatness.

It appears to me that the kind of greatness our Father in Heaven would have us pursue is within the grasp of all who are within the gospel net. We have an unlimited number of opportunities to do the many simple and minor things that will ultimately make us great. To those who have devoted their lives to service and sacrifice for their families, for others, and for the Lord, the best counsel I can give is simply to do more of the same.

To those who are furthering the work of the Lord in so many quiet but significant ways, to those who are the salt of the earth and the strength of the world and the backbone of each nation—to you we would simply express our admiration. If you endure to the end and are valiant in the testimony of Jesus, you will achieve true greatness and will one day live in the presence of our Father in Heaven.

As President Joseph F. Smith has said, "Let us not be trying to substitute an artificial life for the true one." (*Juvenile Instructor,* December 15, 1905, 753.) Let us remember that doing the things that have been ordained by God to be important and needful and necessary, even though the world may view them as unimportant and insignificant, will eventually lead to true greatness.

We should strive to remember the words of the Apostle Paul, especially if we are unhappy with our lives and feeling that we have not achieved some form of greatness. He wrote: "For our light affliction, which is but for a moment, worketh for us a far more exceeding and eternal weight of glory; while we look not at the things which are seen, but at the things which are not seen: for the things which are seen are temporal; but the things which are not seen are eternal." (2 Cor. 4:17–18.)

The small things are significant. We remember not the amount offered by the Pharisee, but the widow's mite; not the power and strength of the Philistine army, but the courage and conviction of David.

May we never be discouraged in doing those daily tasks that God has ordained to be the common lot of man.

Chapter 19

PARENTS' CONCERN FOR CHILDREN

*Parents' hearts are ofttimes broken, yet they
must realize that the ultimate responsibility
lies with the child after parents have
taught correct principles.*

General Authorities have the privilege of meeting and getting acquainted with members of the Church all over the world
who have consistently lived good lives and raised their families
in the influence of the gospel. These Saints have enjoyed the great
blessings and comfort that can come from looking back, as parents, grandparents, and great-grandparents, over long and successful parenting efforts. Surely this is something each of us
would like.

However, there are many in the Church and in the world
who are living with feelings of guilt and unworthiness because
some of their sons and daughters have wandered or strayed from
the fold. We understand that conscientious parents try their best,
yet nearly all make mistakes. One does not launch into such a
project as parenthood without soon realizing that there will be
many errors along the way. Surely our Heavenly Father knows,
when he entrusts his spirit children into the care of young and
inexperienced parents, that there will be mistakes and errors in
judgment.

For every set of parents, there are many first-time experiences that help to build wisdom and understanding, but each such experience results from the plowing of new ground, with the possibility that errors might be made. With the arrival of the first child, the parents must make decisions about how to teach and train, how to correct and discipline. Soon there is the first day at school, and the first bicycle. Then follows the first date of the first teenager, the first problem with school grades, and possibly the first request to stay out late or to buy a car.

It is a rare parent indeed who travels the difficult path of parenting without making errors along the way, especially at these first-time milestones when experience and understanding are somewhat lacking. Even after a parent has gained experience, the second-time and third-time occurrences of these milestones are sometimes not much easier to handle, nor do they come with much less chance of error.

What more challenging responsibility is there than working effectively with young people? There are numerous variables that determine the character and the personality of a child. It is probably true that parents are, in many or perhaps most cases, the greatest influence in shaping the life of a child, but sometimes other influences are also very significant. No one knows the degree to which heredity influences lives, but certainly brothers and sisters, friends and teachers, neighbors and Scoutmasters have significant effects.

We know too that the influences on a child are not restricted to heredity or to people; certainly, things in the physical surroundings will have their effect—such as the house and the playthings, the yard and the neighborhood. Playgrounds and basketballs, dresses and cars—or the lack of these—all have an influence on the child.

With the multitude of influences and the innumerable decisions, each with so many alternatives to consider and evaluate, one must conclude that even though parents strive to choose wisely, an unwise choice will sometimes be made. It is almost impossible to always say and do the right thing at every point along the way. I think we would agree that as parents we have made mistakes that have had negative effects on the attitudes of our children or on their progress. On the other hand, parents usually do the right thing or make the right decision under the circumstances, yet boys and girls often have negative responses to right or correct decisions.

If a parent has made what could be considered an error, or, on the other hand, has never made a mistake but still the lamb has wandered from the fold, there are several thoughts I would like to share.

First, such a father or mother is not alone. Our first parents knew the pain and suffering of seeing some of their children reject the teachings of eternal life. (See Moses 5:27.) Centuries later Jacob came to know of the jealousy and ill feelings of his older sons toward his beloved Joseph. (See Gen. 37:1–8.) The great prophet Alma, who had a son named Alma, prayed to the Lord at length regarding the rebellious attitude of his son and no doubt was overwhelmed with concern and worry about the dissension and the wickedness his son was causing among those who were within the Church. (See Mosiah 27:14.) Our Father in Heaven has also lost many of his spirit children to the world; he knows the feelings of parents' hearts.

Second, we should remember that errors of judgment are generally less serious than errors of intent.

Third, even if a mistake was made with full knowledge and understanding, there is the principle of repentance for release and comfort. Rather than constantly dwelling on what we perceive as a mistake or a sin or a failure to the detriment of our progress in the gospel or our association with family and friends, it would be better for us to turn away from it. As with any mistake, we may repent by being sorrowful and by attempting to correct or rectify the consequences, to whatever extent possible. We should look forward with renewed faith.

Fourth, we must not give up hope for a child who has strayed. Many who have appeared to be completely lost have

113

returned. We must be prayerful and, if possible, let our children know of our love and concern.

Fifth, we need to remember that ours was not the only influence that contributed to the actions of our children, whether those actions were good or bad.

Sixth, our Heavenly Father will recognize the love and the sacrifice, the worry, and the concern, even though great effort has been unsuccessful. Parents' hearts are ofttimes broken, yet we must realize that the ultimate responsibility lies with the child after we have taught correct principles.

Seventh, whatever the sorrow, whatever the concern, whatever the pain and anguish, we must look for a way to turn it to beneficial use—perhaps in helping others to avoid the same problems, or by developing a greater insight into the feelings of others who are struggling in a similar way. Surely we will have a deeper understanding of the love of our Heavenly Father when, through prayer, we finally come to know that he understands and wants us to look forward.

The eighth and final point of reminder is that everyone is different. Each of us is unique. Each child is unique. Just as each of us starts at a different point in the race of life, and just as each of us has different strengths and weaknesses and talents, so each child is blessed with his own special set of characteristics. We must not assume that the Lord will judge the success of one in precisely the same way as another. As parents we often assume that, if our children do not become overachievers in every way, we have failed. We should be careful in our judgments.

Let us not misunderstand. The responsibilities of parenthood are of the greatest importance. The results of our efforts will have eternal consequences for us and the children we raise. All who become parents are under strict obligation to protect and love their children and assist them to return to their Heavenly Father. All parents should understand that the Lord will not hold guiltless those who neglect these responsibilities.

After the Exodus and while Israel was in the wilderness, Moses, in teaching his people, instructed them that the commandments of the Lord should be taught by parents to their children in the home. He said to them: "And these words, which I command thee this day, shall be in thine heart: and thou shalt teach them diligently unto thy children, and shalt talk of them when thou sittest in thine house, and when thou walkest by the way, and when thou liest down, and when thou risest up." (Deut. 6:6–7.)

We should never let Satan fool us into thinking that all is lost. Let us take pride in the good and right things we have done; reject and cast out of our lives those things that are wrong; look to the Lord for forgiveness, strength, and comfort; and then move onward.

A successful parent is one who has loved, one who has sacrificed, and one who has cared for, taught, and ministered to the needs of a child. If you have done all of these and your child is still wayward or troublesome or worldly, it could well be that you are, nevertheless, a successful parent. Perhaps there are children who have come into the world that would challenge any set of parents under any set of circumstances. Likewise, perhaps there are others who would bless the lives of, and be a joy to, almost any father or mother.

My concern is that there are parents who may be pronouncing harsh judgments upon themselves and may be allowing these feelings to destroy their lives, when in fact they have done their best and should continue in faith. That all who are parents might find joy in their efforts with their children is my prayer.

Chapter 20

BLESSED FROM ON HIGH

*Perhaps no promise in life is more reassuring
than the promise of divine assistance and
spiritual guidance in times of need.*

All of us face times in our lives when we need heavenly help in a special and urgent way. We all have moments when we are overwhelmed by circumstances or confused by the counsel we get from others, and we feel a great need to receive spiritual guidance, a great need to find the right path and do the right thing. In the scriptural preface to this latter-day dispensation, the Lord promised that if we would be humble in such times of need and turn to him for aid, we would "be made strong, and [be] blessed from on high, and receive knowledge from time to time." (D&C 1:28.) That help is ours if we will but seek it, trust in it, and follow what King Benjamin, in the Book of Mormon, called "the enticings of the Holy Spirit." (Mosiah 3:19.)

Perhaps no promise in life is more reassuring than that promise of divine assistance and spiritual guidance in times of need. It is a gift freely given from heaven, a gift that we need from our earliest youth through the very latest days of our lives.

Allow me to use three examples of such spiritual experiences, examples that recall the anxious moments of the very

116

young as well as the possibility of continued spiritual growth for those who are not so young.

My first example is the well-known and dearly loved account of the boy-prophet Joseph Smith as he sought to know the mind and will of the Lord at a time of confusion and concern in his life. As every Latter-day Saint knows, the area near Palmyra, New York, had become a place of "unusual excitement on the subject of religion" during young Joseph's boyhood years there. Indeed, the entire district appeared to him to be affected by it, with, he wrote, "great multitudes" uniting themselves to the different religious parties and causing no small "stir and division" among the people. (See JS–H 1:5.)

For a boy who had barely turned fourteen, his search for the truth was made even more difficult and confusing because members of the Smith family differed in their religious preferences at the time.

Now, with that familiar background and setting, I invite you to consider these rather remarkable thoughts and feelings from a boy of such a tender age. He wrote:

"During this time of great excitement my mind was called up to serious reflection and great uneasiness; but though my feelings were deep and often poignant, still I kept myself aloof from all these [factions]   ; so great were the confusion and strife among the different denominations, that it was impossible for a person young as I was, and so unacquainted with men and things, to come to any certain conclusion who was right and who was wrong.

"My mind at times was greatly excited, the cry and tumult were so great and incessant. . . .

"In the midst of this war of words and tumult of opinions, I often said to myself: What is to be done? Who of all these parties are right; or, are they all wrong together? If any one of them be right, which is it, and how shall I know it?

"While I was laboring under the extreme difficulties caused by the contests of these parties of religionists, I was one day reading the Epistle of James, first chapter and fifth verse, which reads:

If any of you lack wisdom, let him ask of God, that giveth to all men liberally, and upbraideth not; and it shall be given him.

"Never did any passage of scripture come with more power to the heart of man than this did at this time to mine. It seemed to enter with great force into every feeling of my heart. I reflected on it again and again, knowing that if any person needed wisdom from God, I did; for how to act I did not know, and unless I could get more wisdom than I then had, I would never know." (JS–H 1:8–12.)

Of course, what happened next changed the course of human history. Determining to "ask of God," young Joseph retired to a grove near his rural home. There, in answer to his fervent prayer, God, the Eternal Father, and his Son, Jesus Christ, visited Joseph and counseled him. That great manifestation, of which I humbly testify, answered many more questions for our dispensation than simply which church young Joseph should or should not join.

But my purpose here is not to outline the first moments of the Restoration, though it is one of the most sacred stories in the scriptures. I wish, rather, simply to emphasize the impressive degree of spiritual sensitivity demonstrated by this young and untutored boy.

How many of us, at fourteen or any age, could keep our heads steady and our wits calm with so many forces tugging and pulling on us, especially on such an important subject as our eternal salvation? How many of us could withstand the emotional conflict that might come when parents differ in their religious persuasions? How many of us, at fourteen or fifty, would search within our souls and search within holy writ to find answers to what the Apostle Paul called "the deep things of God"? (1 Cor. 2:10.)

How remarkable—at least it may seem remarkable to us in our day—that this lad would turn profoundly to the scriptures and then to private prayer, perhaps the two greatest sources of spiritual insight and spiritual impression that are available universally to mankind. Certainly he was torn by differing opinions, but he was determined to do the right thing and determined to find the right way. He believed, as you and I must believe, that he could be taught and blessed from on high, as he was.

But, we may say, Joseph Smith was a very special spirit, and his was a special case. What about the rest of us who may now be older—at least older than fourteen—and have not been destined to open a dispensation of the gospel? We also must make decisions and sort out confusion and cut through a war of words in a whole host of subjects that affect our lives. The world is full of such difficult decisions, and sometimes as we face them, we may feel our age or our infirmities.

Sometimes we may feel that our spiritual edge has grown dull. On some very trying days, we may even feel that God has forgotten us, has left us alone in our confusion and concern. But that feeling is no more justified for the older ones among us than it is for the younger and less experienced. God knows and loves us all. We are, every one of us, his daughters and his sons, and whatever life's lessons may have brought us, the promise is still true: "If any of you lack wisdom, let him ask of God, that giveth to all men liberally, and upbraideth not; and it shall be given him." (James 1:5.)

For my second example, may I refer to one not nearly as young as Joseph Smith. Listen to these lines written by Elizabeth Lloyd Howell when she considered in her poem "Milton's Prayer for Patience" how the majestic poet John Milton must have felt when he went blind late in life:

> I am old and blind!
> Men point at me as smitten by God's frown:
> Afflicted and deserted of my kind,
> Yet am I not cast down.
>
> I am weak, yet strong;
> I murmur not that I no longer see;
> Poor, old, and helpless, I the more belong,
> Father supreme, to thee! . . .

Thy glorious face
Is leaning toward me; and its holy light
Shines in upon my lonely dwelling place,—
And there is no more night.

On my bended knee
I recognize thy purpose clearly shown:
My vision thou hast dimmed, that I may see
Thyself, thyself alone.

"My vision thou hast dimmed, that I may see/Thyself, thyself alone." That is a wonderfully comforting thought to young and old alike who must look inward and upward when the external world around us is so confusing and unstable and grim. Joseph Smith's view of what to do was certainly a dim one until he found the illumination of the scriptures and the searchlight of prayer.

Obviously, it was important to God's purposes that young Joseph was *not* able to see too clearly amidst the confusion caused by men, lest that half-light keep him from seeking and beholding the source of all light and all truth. Like Mrs. Howell's reference to Milton, the blind poet, "on bended knee" we can all recognize God's "purpose clearly shown" if we will rely on spiritual resources, letting our age and experience—yes, and even our infirmities—turn us closer to God.

There may be so very much our Father in Heaven would like to give us—young, old, or middle-aged—if we would but seek his presence regularly through such avenues as scripture study and earnest prayer. Of course, developing spirituality and attuning ourselves to the highest influences of godliness are not an easy matter. It takes time and frequently involves a struggle.

Let me close with a third example noting just such a struggle shared by a youth and an older man.

Elisha, a prophet, seer, and revelator, had counseled the king of Israel on how and where and when to defend against the warring Syrians. The king of Syria, of course, wished to rid his army of Elisha's prophetic interference. The record reads: "Therefore sent he thither horses, and chariots, and a great host: and they came by night, and compassed the city about. . . . [They] compassed the city both with horses and chariots." (2 Kgs. 6:14–15.)

The odds were staggering. It was an old man and a boy against what looked like the whole world. Elisha's young companion was fearful and cried, "Alas, my master! how shall we do?" And Elisha's reply? "Fear not: for they that be with us are more than they that be with them." But there were no others with the old man and his young companion. From what source could their help possibly come?

Then Elisha turned his eyes heavenward, saying, "Lord, I pray thee, open his eyes, that he may see." And, we read, "the Lord opened the eyes of the young man; and he saw: and, behold, the mountain was full of horses and chariots of fire round about Elisha." (2 Kgs. 6:15–17.)

In the gospel of Jesus Christ, we have help from on high. "Be of good cheer," the Lord says, "for I will lead you along." (D&C 78:18.) "I will impart unto you of my Spirit, which shall enlighten your mind, which shall fill your soul with joy." (D&C 11:13.)

I testify of the divinity of Jesus Christ. God does live, and he imparts to us his Spirit. In facing life's problems and meeting life's tasks, may we all claim that gift from God, our Father, and find spiritual joy.

Chapter 21

THE OPENING AND CLOSING OF DOORS

If we are called to pass through tribulation, it
is for our growth and experience and will
ultimately be counted for our good.

Life—every life—has a full share of ups and downs. Indeed, we see many joys and sorrows in the world, many changed plans and new directions, many blessings that do not always look or feel like blessings, and much that humbles us and improves our patience and our faith. We have all had those experiences from time to time, and I suppose we always will.

A passage from one of the greatest prophetic sermons ever given, King Benjamin's masterful discourse to the people of Zarahemla in the Book of Mormon, reads this way:

"Men drink damnation to their own souls except they humble themselves and become as little children. . . . For the natural man is an enemy to God, and has been from the fall of Adam, and will be, forever and ever, unless he yields to the enticings of the Holy Spirit, and putteth off the natural man and becometh a saint through the atonement of Christ the Lord, and becometh as a child, submissive, meek, humble, patient, full of love, willing to submit to all things which the Lord seeth fit to inflict upon him, even as a child doth submit to his father." (Mosiah 3:18–19.)

Being childlike and submitting to our Father's will is not always easy. President Spencer W. Kimball, who knew a good deal about suffering, disappointment, and circumstances beyond his control, once wrote:

"Being human, we would expel from our lives physical pain and mental anguish and assure ourselves of continual ease and comfort, but if we were to close the doors upon sorrow and distress, we might be excluding our greatest friends and benefactors. Suffering can make saints of people as they learn patience, long-suffering, and self-mastery." (*Faith Precedes the Miracle* [Salt Lake City: Deseret Book, 1972], 98.)

In that statement, President Kimball refers to closing doors upon certain experiences in life. That image brings to mind a line from Cervantes' great classic, *Don Quixote*, that has given me comfort over the years. In that masterpiece, we find the short but very important reminder that where one door closes, another opens. Doors close regularly in our lives, and some of those closings cause genuine pain and heartache. But I *do* believe that where one such door closes, another opens (and perhaps more than one), with hope and blessings in other areas of our lives that we might not have discovered otherwise.

President Marion G. Romney had some doors swing closed for him even in the work of his ministry. He knew considerable pain and discouragement. But it was he who said that all men and women, including the most faithful and loyal, would find adversity and affliction in their lives because, in the words of Joseph Smith, "Men have to suffer that they may come upon Mount Zion and be exalted above the heavens." (*History of the Church* 5:556.)

President Romney then explained: "This does not mean that we crave suffering. We avoid all we can. However, we now know, and we all knew when we elected to come into mortality, that we would here be proved in the crucible of adversity and affliction. . . . The Father's plan for proving [and refining] his children did not exempt the Savior himself. The suffering he undertook to endure, and which he did endure, equaled the

123

combined suffering of all men [and women]. . . . He spoke of it as being so intense that it 'caused myself, even God, the greatest of all, to tremble because of pain, and to bleed at every pore, and to suffer both body and spirit—and would that I might not drink the bitter cup, and shrink—nevertheless, . . . I partook and finished my preparations unto the children of men.' (D&C 19:18–19.)" (Conference Report, October 1969, 57.)

All of us must finish our "preparations unto the children of men." Christ's preparations were quite different from our own, but we all have preparations to make, doors to open. To make such important preparations often requires some pain, some unexpected changes in life's path, and some submitting, "even as a child doth submit to his father." Finishing divine preparations and opening celestial doors may take us—indeed, undoubtedly will take us—right up to the concluding hours of our mortal lives.

Elder A. Theodore Tuttle recently opened a new door to return to his heavenly home. His preparations in mortality had been fully completed for such a journey. He too, like President Romney, spoke of adversity that he knew would come to each of us but that he may not then have known would come to him as early as it did. In general conference in 1967 he said:

"Adversity, in one form or another, is the universal experience of man. It is the common lot of all . . . to experience misfortune, suffering, sickness, or other adversities. Ofttimes our work is arduous and unnecessarily demanding. Our faith is tried in various ways—sometimes [it seems] unjustly tried. At times it seems that even God is punishing us and ours. One of the things that makes all this so hard to bear is that we ourselves appear to be chosen for this affliction while others presumably escape these adversities. . . . [But] we cannot indulge ourselves the luxury of self-pity." (Conference Report, October 1967, 14–15.)

Elder Tuttle then left us these lines from Robert Browning Hamilton titled "Along the Road," which teach a lesson on pleasure and a lesson on sorrow:

124

I walked a mile with Pleasure.
She chattered all the way,
But left me none the wiser
For all she had to say.

I walked a mile with Sorrow,
And ne'er a word said she;
But, oh, the things I learned from her
When Sorrow walked with me!

And now this mortal portion of Elder Tuttle's journey is over. He closed that door and opened another. Now he walks and talks with the angels. And so, someday, will we close and open those same doors.

I have mentioned the lives of two of our contemporary brethren. Obviously, prophets of an earlier day have known adversity and difficulty as well. They were not spared these challenges any more than our generation has been spared. The great Book of Mormon patriarch Lehi spoke encouragingly to his son Jacob, a son born in the wilderness in a time of travail and opposition. Jacob's life was not as he might have expected it to be and not as the ideal course of experience might have outlined. He had suffered afflictions and setbacks, but Lehi promised that such afflictions would be consecrated for his son's gain. Then Lehi added these words that have become classic:

"For it must needs be, that there is an opposition in all things. If not so, . . . righteousness could not be brought to pass, neither wickedness, neither holiness nor misery, neither good nor bad." (2 Ne. 2:2, 11.)

I have taken great comfort over the years in this explanation of some of life's pain and disappointment. I take even greater comfort that the greatest of men and women, including the Son of God, have faced such opposition in order to better understand the contrast between righteousness and wickedness, holiness and misery, good and bad. Within the dark, damp confinement of Liberty Jail, the Prophet Joseph Smith learned that if we are called to pass through tribulation, it is for our growth and experience and will ultimately be counted for our good. (See D&C 122:5–8.)

Where one door shuts, another opens, even for a prophet in prison. We are not always wise enough nor experienced enough to judge adequately all the possible entries and exits. The mansion that God prepares for each of his beloved children may have only certain hallways and banisters, special carpets and curtains that he would have us pass on our way to possess it.

I share the view expressed by Orson F. Whitney: "No pain that we suffer, no trial that we experience is wasted. It ministers to our education, to the development of such qualities as patience, faith, fortitude and humility. All that we suffer and all that we endure, especially when we endure it patiently, builds up our characters, purifies our hearts, expands our souls, and makes us more tender and charitable, more worthy to be called the children of God . . . and it is through sorrow and suffering, toil and tribulation, that we gain the education that we come here to acquire and which will make us more like our Father and Mother in heaven." (Quoted in Kimball, *Faith Precedes the Miracle*, 98.)

At various times in our lives, probably at repeated times in our lives, we have to acknowledge that God knows what we do not know and sees what we do not see. "For my thoughts are not your thoughts, neither are your ways my ways, saith the Lord." (Isa. 55:8.)

If you have troubles at home with children who stray, if you suffer financial reverses and emotional strain that threaten your home and your happiness, if you must face the loss of life or health, may peace be unto your soul. We will not be tempted beyond our ability to withstand. Our detours and disappointments are the straight and narrow path to Him, as we sing in one of our favorite hymns:

> *When through fiery trials thy pathway shall lie,*
> *My grace, all sufficient, shall be thy supply.*

The flame shall not hurt thee; I only design
Thy dross to consume and thy gold to refine.
—Hymns, *no. 85*

May God bless us in the ups and downs of life, in the opening and closing of doors.

Part 4

BECOMING
DISCIPLES OF CHRIST

*"And all saints who remember to keep and do
these sayings, walking in obedience to the
commandments, . . . shall find wisdom
and great treasures of knowledge,
even hidden treasures."*
(D&C 89:18–19)

Chapter 22

GOSPEL IMPERATIVES

*The gospel of Jesus Christ is full of
imperatives, words that call for personal
commitment and action.*

The greatest search of our time is the search for personal identity and for human dignity. Each of us wants life to be worthwhile and to have real meaning—a personal meaning—in the living we do from day to day. There is a search being made by people everywhere, a search as important as life itself for self-respect, for self-fulfillment, and for emotional maturity. Much of our character and nature, as individuals, depends upon how and to what ends we conduct this search. Too many of us turn the direction of our lives to tragic goals and distorted purposes. The friends we choose, the choices we make, and what we do about these choices are the determining guidelines that form and mold our lives, but choices alone are not enough. The best goals, the best of friends, and the best of opportunities are all meaningless unless they are translated into reality through our daily actions.

Belief must be realized in personal achievement. Real Christians must understand that the gospel of Jesus Christ is not just a gospel of belief; it is a plan of action. His gospel is a gospel of imperatives, and the very nature of its substance is a call to action. He did not say, "Observe my gospel"; he said, "Live it!"

He did not say, "Note its beautiful structure and imagery"; he said, "Go, do, see, feel, give, believe!" The gospel of Jesus Christ is full of imperatives, words that call for personal commitment and action—obligatory, binding, compulsory.

There is never achievement in any field of endeavor unless it is preceded by a strong sense of purpose. There must be reasons for action and guides for action in the form of real goals and objectives. That is why we are given a plan of salvation and progression. Because the gospel is a long-range—even an eternal—goal, it must be broken up into short-range, immediate objectives that can be achieved today and tomorrow and the next day. The gospel imperatives constitute an immediate challenge to action in our lives right now, today, as well as a plan for action eternally.

Notice the forceful expression Jesus gave to his teachings:

"Ask, and it shall be given you; seek, and ye shall find; knock, and it shall be opened unto you: For every one that asketh receiveth; and he that seeketh findeth; and to him that knocketh it shall be opened." (Matt. 7:7–8.)

"Love your enemies, bless them that curse you, do good to them that hate you, and pray for them that despitefully use you." (Matt. 5:44.)

I believe he would have endorsed the modern addition to an ancient scripture: "And with all thy getting, get going!" His principles are briefly paraphrased: "*Do* unto others as you would have them *do* unto you." "*Go* the second mile." "If you want to know whether what I say is true, try it out!" This is what we mean by gospel imperatives. They are words that challenge to action—go, do, pray, repent, love, find, give, consider, provide, and a host of others.

One of the most dynamic challenges in the scriptures comes at the end of King Benjamin's address to his people as he concludes his ministry and turns the reins of government over to his son Mosiah. Standing on the tower he built to address the people, he guides them through the fundamentals of the gospel and commits them to the wisdom, power, and purposes of God, making this most important challenge: "and now, if you believe all these things see that ye do them." (Mosiah 4:10.) The sincerity of their belief must be demonstrated in the verity of their actions.

Action is one of the chief foundations of personal testimony. The surest witness is that which comes firsthand out of personal experience. When the Jews challenged the doctrine Jesus taught in the temple, he answered, "My doctrine is not mine, but his that sent me." Then he added the key to personal testimony: "If any man will do his will, he shall know of the doctrine, whether it be of God, or whether I speak of myself." (John 7:16–17.)

Do we hear the imperative in this declaration of the Savior? "If any man will *do*, . . . he will *know!*" John caught the significance of this imperative and emphasized its meaning in his writings. He said, "He that saith he abideth in him ought himself also so to walk, even as he walked." (1 Jn. 2:6.)

Merely saying, accepting, and believing are not enough. They are incomplete until that which they imply is translated into the dynamic action of daily living. This, then, is the finest source of personal testimony. We know because we have experienced. We do not have to say, "Brother Jones says it is true, and I believe him." We can say, "I have lived this principle in my own life, and I know through personal experience that it works. I have felt its influence, tested its practical usefulness, and know that it is good. I can testify of my own knowledge that it is a true principle."

Many people carry such a testimony in their own lives and do not recognize its worth. Recently a young lady said, "I do not have a testimony of the gospel. I wish I did. I accept its teachings. I know they work in my life. I see them working in the lives of others. If only the Lord would answer my prayers and give me a testimony, I would be one of the happiest persons alive." What this young lady wanted was a miraculous intervention; yet she had already seen the miracle of the gospel enlarging and uplifting her own life. The Lord *had* answered her prayers. She *did* have a testimony, but she did not recognize it for what it was. Of such, Jesus said, "They seeing see not; and hearing they hear not, neither do they understand. And in them is fulfilled the

133

prophecy of Esaias, which saith, By hearing and seeing ye shall see, and shall not perceive." (Matt. 13:13–14.)

The gospel is the way of life. It is practical, plain, and simple. It is a gospel of action, even to the tiny day-to-day actions that make up the art of living.

Elder Adam S. Bennion used to say, "Important as knowing is, there is a more important field, and that is the field of doing. Life is always bigger than learning. It is a wonderful thing to know, but it is better to do." This, of course, is the meaning of the biblical injunction, "Be ye doers of the word, and not hearers only" (James 1:22), which is another gospel imperative.

This gospel imperative expresses the very nature of Church education. The doctrine of making hearers into doers of the word extends to the point at which we believe that what we know and do in the gospel needs to become ingrained into the very nature of our being. Nels L. Nelson expressed this gospel imperative in one of his books defining the Mormon concept of education: "The only kind of education which squares with the ideals of Mormonism is that which trains a man to do. If it be asked, to do what, the answer is, *to do the things that need to be done*. . . . True education is therefore training a man to do his part in the social world. . . .

"Knowledge is only half of intelligence. To stop here is to be falsely educated. If, however, the truth perceived becomes a dynamic fact in a man's character; if it is incorporated into his mental attitude, and reacts immediately upon his life; if, in short, it ceases to be something *in* a man, and becomes the man himself, changing the very . . . [character] of his soul, then knowledge has passed over into power—or character—or wisdom—or, to adopt the term used by Joseph Smith, has passed over into intelligence; and it is such a process alone that represents true education." (*Scientific Aspects of Mormonism* [New York and London: G. P. Putnam's Sons, 1904], 151–52.)

If the gospel of Jesus Christ is truly to become a part of ourselves, then there are several things we must keep in mind in putting the gospel imperatives into action.

First, it is essential to remember that it is more important to be able to *think* and hence to *act* in terms of gospel principles and teachings than it is to merely memorize gospel facts. Remember the injunction from Proverbs: "Wisdom is the principal thing; therefore get wisdom: and with all thy getting get understanding." (Prov. 4:7.) Solomon's great blessing was "an understanding heart." We should study gospel principles with the purpose of understanding how they apply and may be used in our life today, not just be able to remember them.

Second, don't be afraid to put them into action. Courage—and this is as true of spiritual courage as it is of physical courage—is not acting in the absence of fear. Courage is acting in spite of fear. If we stood tall in the gospel, we would soon find that it is easier to act than it is to remain idle or to cower in a corner.

Third, remember that our attitudes are most important tools to success. Knowledge is power only when it is used constructively. We should extend a positive belief in our own ability to live the gospel as an effective factor in our lives and in the lives of those about us. Businessmen have proven that the difference between the successful and the unsuccessful usually reduces down to a difference in attitudes. This is just as true of gospel living. "An [a man] thinketh in his heart, so is he" ought to be a prime tenet in every gospel lesson. (Prov. 23:7.)

Fourth, be assured that one kind of ability we must have is "stick-ability." No matter how good the beginning, success comes only to those who "endure to the end."

Fifth, whenever we tackle a gospel imperative, immediate goals will help us master it. Our decision to read scripture becomes quite practical when we decide to read a chapter at night before we go to sleep. We should set up long-range and eternal goals, to be sure—they will be the guides and inspiration of a lifetime; but we should not forget the countless little immediate objectives to be won tomorrow and tomorrow and tomorrow. To win and pass these objectives marks our progress toward

135

the greater goals and ensures happiness and the feelings of success along the way.

Gospel imperatives are action words challenging every Latter-day Saint to gospel living. They are the active pathway to personal participation in the laws of the gospel, and every one leads to rewards and blessings. An example of this may be found in the blessing attached to one of these gospel imperatives. It reads, "And all saints who remember to keep and do these sayings, walking in obedience to the commandments, shall receive health in their navel and marrow to their bones; and shall find wisdom and great treasures of knowledge, even hidden treasures." (D&C 89:18–19.) Such are the blessings promised, and there are many more, each to its own gospel imperative. They are imperatives because they call to action, and every positive action in the gospel plan makes better and happier men and women.

I never think of gospel imperatives without remembering the story of Mary Fielding Smith, that indomitable pioneer mother who was the wife and widow of the Patriarch Hyrum Smith, brother of the Prophet. I am sure you are all familiar with the story of her struggles to bring her little family to the valley of the Great Salt Lake. One of the highlights in that story for me is also the signature of gospel imperatives.

One spring as the family opened their potato pits, she had her sons get a load of the best potatoes to take to the tithing office.

She was met at the steps of the office by one of the clerks, who remonstrated as the boys began to unload the potatoes. "Widow Smith," he said, remembering no doubt her trials and sacrifices, "it's a shame that you should have to pay tithing." He added a number of other things her son Joseph did not care to repeat, chided her for paying her tithing, and called her anything but wise and prudent, adding that others able to work were supported from the tithing office.

The little widow drew herself up to her full height and said, "William, you ought to be ashamed of yourself. Would you deny me a blessing? If I did not pay my tithing I should expect the

Lord to withhold His blessings from me; I pay my tithing, not only because it is a law of God but because I expect a blessing by doing it. By keeping this and other laws, I expect to prosper and to be able to provide for my family." (Joseph Fielding Smith, *Life of Joseph F. Smith* [Salt Lake City, 1938], 158–59.)

This is the goal of gospel imperatives, to be able to prosper and provide for our families. The abundance of the good and worthwhile things of life comes from following them. I bear you my testimony that in them lies the wisdom of eternity. May we catch the vision of and follow the admonition contained in the key to all imperatives: "For every one that asketh, receiveth; and he that seeketh, findeth; and to him that knocketh, it shall be opened." (3 Ne. 14:8.)

Chapter 23

THE PHARISEE
AND THE PUBLICAN

The Pharisee asked nothing of God, but relied
upon his own self-righteousness. The publican
appealed to God for mercy and forgiveness.

"Two men went up into the temple to pray; the one a Pharisee, and the other a publican." (Luke 18:10.)

These words begin one of the many stories told by the Master Teacher during the three years of his earthly ministry. There is nothing in all literature equal to the parables of Christ. His teachings were as impressive to his listeners then as they are to those who read his words today. They are so simple that a child can understand, yet profound enough for the sage and philosopher. The similitudes he used were taken from pictures of human life and commonplace incidents that could be understood by every listener—the sower, the lost sheep, a woman baking bread, the fig tree, a good Samaritan, the prodigal son.

Each of the parables spoken by the Savior seems to teach a principle or give an admonition regarding the attributes necessary to qualify for exaltation. Some of these are faith, repentance, baptism, development of talents, forgiveness, perseverance in doing good, being a profitable steward, charity, mercy, and obedience. These parables were usually given by him to add to the knowledge of persons already spiritually enlightened, particularly the disciples, although they were sometimes directed to other persons and audiences.

The parable from which I read the first verse was directed to more than just his disciples. Even though the subject matter was a Pharisee and a publican, it was not intended for Pharisees or publicans expressly, but for the benefit of the self-righteous who lack the virtues of humility and who use self-righteousness as a claim to exaltation. In this parable the Savior spoke few words, yet the lesson taught is clear. This is the whole story he told, as recorded by Luke:

"Two men went up into the temple to pray; the one a Pharisee, and the other a publican.

"The Pharisee stood and prayed thus with himself, God, I thank thee, that I am not as other men are, extortioners, unjust, adulterers, or even as this publican. I fast twice in the week, I give tithes of all that I possess.

"And the publican, standing afar off, would not lift up so much as his eyes unto heaven, but smote upon his breast, saying, God be merciful to me a sinner.

"I tell you, this man went down to his house justified rather than the other: for every one that exalteth himself shall be abased; and he that humbleth himself shall be exalted." (Luke 18:10–14.)

Apparently the scene is laid in Jerusalem at the temple, where two men had gone to pray during the time of day for private prayers. It is interesting that the Master selected a Pharisee and a publican as the actors in the story, representing the two religious extremes in Jewish society.

The Pharisees were the largest and most influential of the three sects of Judaism at the time of Christ. The pharisaic movement in the Jewish state rose from the ranks of the lay lawyers of the Greek period to become the leading religious and political party. The main characteristics of the Pharisees were their legalism and their legalistic inflexibility. They were known for their strict accuracy in interpreting the law and their scrupulous adherence to living the law in every minute detail. This caused them to be known as the strictest of Jewish sects in observing their tradition. They shunned the non-Pharisee as being unclean, thereby keeping themselves separated from those they considered to be the common people.

Paul was a Pharisee, the son of a Pharisee, and he was educated by Gamaliel, a Pharisee. On three different occasions he declared himself to be a member of the sect. The first was at the time he was on trial, then in his plea before Agrippa, and later in writing to the Philippians. This training as a Pharisee made him an extremist in his devotion to the Jewish law, which answers the question as to why he was such a zealous persecutor of the Christians prior to his experience on Damascus Road.

Publicans were tax collectors and were looked down upon with contempt. Ordinary taxes, such as land taxes, were collected by the Roman officials; but toll taxes for transporting goods were usually collected by Jews under contract with the Romans. These collectors, or publicans, made a profit on the transactions. Their fellow countrymen had no higher regard for them than for thieves and robbers. The trade lent itself to graft and extortion, and the publicans had the reputation of having some of the tax money stick to their own fingers.

The Jews were smarting under Roman occupation and domination, and they considered the payment of taxes as a tribute to Caesar. Jews who made such collections for the Romans were regarded as traitors and as despicable for selling their services to a foreign conqueror. Publicans and members of their families were considered so contemptible that they were not allowed to hold public office or give testimony in a Jewish court. We remember that Matthew was a publican, a gatherer of taxes, until his calling to be a disciple, and, of course, he too was despised by the Jews, as were the others who followed that occupation.

To know the background of these two men who came from the opposite extremes of Jewish society helps us to understand this parable of the Pharisee and tax collector and why they prayed as they did in the temple.

After the two men entered the temple, the Pharisee stood by

himself, apart from the tax collector, and thanked God that he was "not as other men are, extortioners, unjust, adulterers" who fail to live the commandments of the law, "or even as this publican," he said. Though he was in form thanking God, his self-centered thoughts were on his own self-righteousness. In justification he added: "I fast twice in the week, I give tithes of all that I possess." (Luke 18:11–12.) His prayer was not one of thankfulness, but of boastfulness.

The boastful spirit and pride of this Pharisee is not unlike that of Rabbi Simeon ben Jochai, mentioned in the Talmud, who said: "If there were only thirty righteous persons in the world, I and my son should make two of them; but if there were but twenty, I and my son would be of the number; and if there were but ten, I and my son would be of the number; and if there were but five, I and my son would be of the five; and if there were but two, I and my son would be those two; and if there were but one, myself should be that one." (Bereshith Rabba, s. 35, vol. 34.)

The tax collector standing afar off, feeling the weight of his iniquities pressing down upon him, and being conscious of his sins and unworthiness to stand before God, cast his eyes to the ground and "would not lift up so much as his eyes unto heaven" when he prayed. In deep distress he beat upon his breast and pleaded, "God be merciful to me a sinner." (Luke 18:13.)

Could there be greater contrast in the prayers of two men? The Pharisee stood apart because he believed he was better than other men, whom he considered as common. The publican stood apart also, but it was because he felt himself unworthy. The Pharisee thought of no one other than himself and regarded everyone else a sinner, whereas the publican thought of everyone else as righteous as compared with himself, a sinner. The Pharisee asked nothing of God but relied upon his own self-righteousness. The publican appealed to God for mercy and forgiveness of his sins.

Continuing the story, Jesus then said: "I tell you, this man," referring to the publican, the despised tax collector, "went down to his house justified rather than the other." (Luke 18:14.) In other words, the Lord said he was absolved, forgiven, or vindicated.

This statement gives meaning to what the Savior said on another occasion: "Except your righteousness shall exceed the righteousness of the scribes and Pharisees, ye shall in no case enter into the kingdom of heaven." (Matt. 5:20.)

The Master then concluded the parable with these words: "For every one that exalteth himself shall be abased; and he that humbleth himself shall be exalted." (Luke 18:14.) These are almost the same words he spoke in the house of one of the chief Pharisees. (See Luke 14:11.)

Humility is an attribute of godliness possessed by true Saints. It is easy to understand why a proud man fails. He is content to rely upon himself only. This is evident in those who seek social position or who push others aside to gain position in fields of business, government, education, sports, or other endeavors. Our genuine concern should be for the success of others. The proud man shuts himself off from God, and when he does so, he no longer lives in the light. The Apostle Peter made this comment: "Be clothed with humility: for God resisteth the proud, and giveth grace to the humble. Humble yourselves therefore under the mighty hand of God, that he may exalt you in due time." (1 Pet. 5:5–6.)

From the beginning of time, there have been those with pride and others who have followed divine admonition to be humble. History bears record that those who have exalted themselves have been abased, but the humble have been exalted. On every busy street there are Pharisees and publicans. It may be that one of them bears our name.

May the Lord bless us as we strive to understand and follow his teachings.

142

Chapter 24

THE LORD'S
TOUCHSTONE

*The touchstone of compassion is a measure of
our discipleship; it is a measure of our love for
God and for one another.*

In ancient times, one test of the purity of gold was performed with a smooth, black, siliceous stone called a touchstone. When rubbed across the touchstone, the gold produced a streak or mark on its surface. The goldsmith matched this mark to a color on his chart of graded colors. The mark was redder as the amount of copper or alloy increased or yellower as the percentage of gold increased. This process showed quite accurately the purity of the gold.

The touchstone method of testing the purity of gold was quick and was satisfactory for most practical purposes. But the goldsmith who still questioned the purity completed a more accurate test by using a process that involved fire.

I suggest to you that the Lord has prepared a touchstone for you and me, an outward measurement of inward discipleship that marks our faithfulness and will survive the fires yet to come.

On one occasion while Jesus was teaching the people, a certain lawyer approached him and posed this question: "Master, what shall I do to inherit eternal life?"

Jesus, the Master Teacher, replied to the man, who obviously was well-versed in the law, with a counter-question: "What is written in the law? how readest thou?"

The man replied with resolute summary the two great commandments: "Thou shalt love the Lord thy God with all thy heart, and with all thy soul, and with all thy strength, and with all thy mind; and thy neighbour as thyself."

With approval Christ responded, "This do, and thou shalt live." (Luke 10:25–28.)

Eternal life, God's life, the life we are seeking, is rooted in two commandments. The scriptures say that "on these two commandments hang all the law and the prophets." (Matt. 22:40.) Love God and love your neighbor. The two work together; they are inseparable. In the highest sense they may be considered as synonymous. And they are commandments that each of us can live.

The answer of Jesus to the lawyer might be considered as the Lord's touchstone. He said on another occasion, "Inasmuch as ye have done it unto one of the least of these my brethren, ye have done it unto me." (Matt. 25:40.) He will measure our devotion to him by how we love and serve our fellowmen. What kind of mark are we leaving on the Lord's touchstone? Are we truly good neighbors? Does the test show us to be twenty-four–karat gold, or can the trace of fool's gold be detected?

As if excusing himself for asking such a simple question of the Master, the lawyer sought to justify himself by further inquiring, "And who is my neighbour?" (Luke 10:29.)

We all ought to be eternally grateful for that question, for in the Savior's reply came one of his richest and most appreciated parables, one that each of us has read and heard over and over again:

"A certain man went down from Jerusalem to Jericho, and fell among thieves, which stripped him of his raiment, and wounded him, and departed, leaving him half dead. And by chance there came down a certain priest that way: and when he saw him, he passed by on the other side. And likewise a Levite, when he was at the place, came and looked on him, and passed by on the other side.

"But a certain Samaritan, as he journeyed, came where he was: and when he saw him, he had compassion on him, and went to him, and bound up his wounds, pouring in oil and wine, and set him on his own beast, and brought him to an inn, and took care of him.

"And on the morrow when he departed, he took out two pence, and gave them to the host, and said unto him, Take care of him; and whatsoever thou spendest more, when I come again, I will repay thee." Then Jesus asked the lawyer, "Which now of these three, thinkest thou, was neighbour unto him that fell among the thieves?" (Luke 10:30–36.)

There the Master holds out the touchstone of Christianity. He asks that our mark be measured on it.

Both the priest and the Levite in Christ's parable should have remembered the requirements of the law: "Thou shalt not see thy brother's ass or his ox fall down by the way, and hide thyself from them: thou shalt surely help him to lift them up again." (Deut. 22:4.) And if an ox, how much more should one be willing to help a brother in need. But as Elder James E. Talmage wrote, "Excuses [not to do so] are easy to find; they spring up as readily and plentifully as weeds by the wayside." (*Jesus the Christ*, 1916, 431.)

The Samaritan gave us an example of pure Christian love. He had compassion. He went to the man who had been injured by the thieves and bound up his wounds, took him to an inn, cared for him, paid his expenses, and offered more if needed for his care. This is a story of the love of a neighbor for his neighbor.

An old axiom states that a man "all wrapped up in himself makes a small bundle." Love has a certain way of making a small bundle large. The key is to love our neighbor, including the neighbor who is difficult to love. We need to remember that though we make our friends, God has made our neighbors—everywhere. Love should have no boundary; we should have no narrow loyalties. Christ said, "For if ye love them which love you, what reward have ye? do not even the publicans the same?" (Matt. 5:46.)

Joseph Smith wrote a letter to the Saints, published in the *Messenger and Advocate,* on the subject of loving one another to be justified before God. He wrote:

"Dear Brethren:—It is a duty which every Saint ought to render to his brethren freely—to always love them, and ever succor them. To be justified before God we must love one another: we must overcome evil; we must visit the fatherless and the widow in their affliction, and we must keep ourselves unspotted from the world: for such virtues flow from the great fountain of pure religion. Strengthening our faith by adding every good quality that adorns the children of the blessed Jesus, we can pray in the season of prayer; we can love our neighbor as ourselves, and be faithful in tribulation, knowing that the reward of such is greater in the kingdom of heaven. What a consolation! What a joy! Let me live the life of the righteous, and let my reward be like this!" (*History of the Church* 2:229.)

These two virtues, love and service, are required of us if we are to be good neighbors and find peace in our lives. Surely they were in the heart of Elder Willard Richards. While Elder Richards was in Carthage Jail on the afternoon of the martyrdom of Joseph and Hyrum Smith, the jailer suggested that they would be safer in the cells. Joseph turned to Elder Richards and asked, "If we go into the cell will you go with us?"

Elder Richards's reply was one of love: "Brother Joseph, you did not ask me to cross the river with you—you did not ask me to come to Carthage—you did not ask me to come to jail with you—and do you think I would forsake you now? But I will tell you what I will do; if you are condemned to be hung for 'treason,' I will be hung in your stead, and you shall go free."

It must have been with considerable emotion and feeling that Joseph replied, "But you cannot."

To this Elder Richards firmly answered, "I will." (See B. H. Roberts, *A Comprehensive History of the Church* [Salt Lake City, 1930], 2:283.)

Elder Richards's test was perhaps greater than most of us will face: the test of fire rather than of the touchstone. But if we were asked to do so, could we lay down our lives for our families? our friends? our neighbors?

The touchstone of compassion is a measure of our discipleship; it is a measure of our love for God and for one another. Will we leave a mark of pure gold or, like the priest and the Levite, will we pass by on the other side?

May the Lord bless us in our quest to be true disciples and good neighbors.

Chapter 25

AM I A "LIVING" MEMBER?

*Being a "living" member of the Church means
that we are everyday Christians, walking as
Christ would have us walk.*

At a critical moment in the battle of Waterloo, when everything depended on the steadiness of the soldiery, an anxious courier dashed into the presence of the Duke of Wellington, announcing that unless the troops were immediately relieved or withdrawn, they must yield before the impending assault of the French army. The Duke replied, "Stand firm!"

"But we shall perish," remonstrated the officer.

"Stand firm!" again was the answer of the ironhearted Duke.

"You'll find us there!" rejoined the courier, as he galloped away.

And, of course, the British were victorious that day as a result of such loyalty and determination. (Walter Baxendale, ed., *Dictionary of Anecdote, Incident, Illustrative Fact* [New York, 1889], 225.)

Today another battle of far more serious consequence is being waged. It is a battle being fought for the souls of men. Its outcome likewise depends on the steadiness of the soldiery. The clarion call of the chieftain is heard above the fierce artillery of the archenemy, "Stand firm! Be true!"

I am grateful that most Latter-day Saints today are standing firm and remaining true to the kingdom of God. Like Helaman's stripling warriors, "they stand fast in that liberty wherewith God has made them free; and they are strict to remember the Lord their God from day to day; yea, they do observe to keep his statutes, and his judgments, and his commandments continually; and their faith is strong in the prophecies concerning that which is to come." (Alma 58:40.) I am referring to those members of the Church who live their Christian beliefs in the quiet commonplace of their daily lives.

On November 1, 1831, at a conference of the Church in Hiram, Ohio, the Lord revealed in the preface to the Doctrine and Covenants that this is the "only true and living church upon the face of the whole earth, with which I, the Lord, am well pleased, speaking unto the church collectively and not individually." (D&C 1:30.) This should raise a question in our minds of eternal significance: We know that this is the true and living church institutionally, but am I a true and living member individually?

This question may appear as a play on the words of the Lord when he said this is the true and living church. When I ask, "Am I a true and living member?" my question is, Am I deeply and fully dedicated to keeping the covenants I have made with the Lord? Am I totally committed to living the gospel and being a doer of the word and not a hearer only? Do I live my religion? Will I remain true? Do I stand firm against Satan's temptations? He is seeking to cause us to lose our way in a storm of derision and a tide of sophistry. We can have victory, however, by responding to that inner voice calling "Stand firm!"

To answer affirmatively the question "Am I a living member?" confirms our commitment. It means that we now and always will love God and our neighbors as ourselves. It means that our actions will reflect who we are and what we believe. It means that we are everyday Christians, walking as Christ would have us walk.

Living members are those who strive to have a total commitment. They follow the admonition of Nephi who wrote: "And now, my beloved brethren, after ye have gotten into this strait and narrow path, I would ask if all is done? Behold, I say unto you, Nay; for ye have not come thus far save it were by the word of Christ with unshaken faith in him, relying wholly upon the merits of him who is mighty to save.

"Wherefore, ye must press forward with a steadfastness in Christ, having a perfect brightness of hope, and a love of God and of all men. Wherefore, if ye shall press forward, feasting upon the word of Christ, and endure to the end, behold, thus saith the Father: Ye shall have eternal life." (2 Ne. 31:19–20.)

Living members recognize their duty to press forward. They are baptized as a first step of their living journey. It is a sign to God, to angels, and to heaven that they will follow God's will. We especially welcome those throughout the world who have recently taken upon themselves these covenants. We express our love for them and want them to know of our concern for them and all members everywhere. We welcome them into the brotherhood and sisterhood of the Latter-day Saints. The word *saint* does not mean that any of us is perfect. What it does mean is that we are all trying, all serving, and all vowing to stand firm in the faith.

Living members never stray from the path of their commitment. On one occasion a certain man came to the Savior and said to him: "Lord, I will follow thee; but let me first go bid them farewell, which are at home at my house. And Jesus said unto him, No man, having put his hand to the plough, and looking back, is fit for the kingdom of God." (Luke 9:61–62.)

To dig a straight furrow, the plowman needs to keep his eyes on a fixed point ahead of him. That keeps him on a true course. If, however, he happens to look back to see where he has been, his chances of straying are increased. The results are crooked and irregular furrows. We invite those who are new members to fix their attention on their new goal and never look back on their earlier problems or transgressions except as a reminder of their growth and their worth and their blessings from God. If our energies are focused not behind us but ahead of us—on eternal life and the joy of salvation—we assuredly will obtain it.

Living members give heed to the Spirit, which quickens the inner life. They constantly seek its direction. They pray for strength and overcome difficulties. Their hearts are not set upon the things of this world but upon the infinite. Spiritual renewal is not sacrificed for physical gratification.

Living members put Christ first in their lives, knowing from what source their lives and progress come. There is a tendency for people to put themselves in the center of the universe and expect others to conform to their wants and needs and desires. Yet nature does not honor that erroneous assumption. The central role in life belongs to God. Instead of asking him to do our bidding, we should seek to bring ourselves into harmony with his will, and thus continue our progress as living members.

The first great commandment is: "Love the Lord thy God with all thy heart, and with all thy soul, and with all thy mind." (Matt. 22:37.) In order to love him, we need to do the things he has asked us to do. We need to show that we are willing to become like him.

Living members, once they are converted, fulfill the commandment to strengthen their brothers and sisters. They are anxious to share their joy with others, and they never lose this desire. Patrick Henry said at the closing scene of his life: "I have now disposed of all my property to my family. . . . There is one thing more I wish I could give them, and that is the Christian religion. . . . If they had that, and I had not given them one shilling, they would have been rich, and if they had not that, and I had given them all the world, they would be poor." (*The New Dictionary of Thoughts* [Garden City, New York: Standard Book Co., 1961], 561.)

Living members recognize the need to put into action their beliefs. These Saints are anxiously engaged in bringing to pass many good and noble works of their own free will and accord. President Heber J. Grant once observed that "the power is in us wherein we are agents unto ourselves, and that we should not wait to be commanded in all things, and he that is compelled in all things is a slothful and not a wise servant. We should have the ambition, we should have the desire, we should make up our minds that, so far as the Lord Almighty has given to us talent, we will do our full share in the battle of life. It should be a matter of pride that no man shall do more than you will do, in proportion to your ability, in forwarding the work of God here upon the earth." (*Improvement Era,* October 1939, 585.)

Living members love one another. They visit the fatherless and the widows in their afflictions. They keep themselves unspotted from the world.

As members of the living church, we have a belief in the living God. Prior to crossing the Jordan River, Joshua summoned the children of Israel, saying, "Come hither, and hear the words of the Lord your God. . . . Hereby ye shall know that the living God is among you." (Josh. 3:9–10.) Young David, in response to Goliath's challenge, courageously said to the men near him, "Who is this uncircumcised Philistine, that he should defy the armies of the living God?" (1 Sam. 17:26.) Jeremiah likewise referred to the Lord as the true and living God. (See Jer. 10:10.)

We have a firm belief in the statement that this is the true and living church of the true and living God. The question we have yet to answer is: Am I dedicated and committed, a true and living member?

May we stand firm and be true and living members of the Church and receive the promised reward to be among those spoken of in the Doctrine and Covenants "who are come unto Mount Zion, and unto the city of the living God, the heavenly place, the holiest of all." (D&C 76:66.)

Chapter 26

OUR COMMITMENT
TO GOD

*Experiences in the life of Joshua are
instructive to us regarding the importance
of keeping commitments and following
the Lord's commandments.*

Reading and studying the scriptures makes us conscious of the many conditional promises made by the Lord to encourage obedience and righteous living. Israelite history is filled with examples of covenants, which constitute one of the central themes of the Old Testament—the promises of God made in exchange for the commitments of the prophets and the people.

The Lord made a covenant with Noah, and the rainbow became the token of that eternal covenant with all mankind. (See Gen. 9:13.) The covenant made with Abraham and his seed was sealed by the ceremony of circumcision as a sacrament. (See Gen. 17:10–11.) And the token or sign of the great covenant with all Israel made at Sinai was the Sabbath. (See Ex. 31:12–17.)

Several experiences in the life of Joshua are instructive to us today regarding the importance placed by the Lord on keeping commitments and on being committed to following the commandments and direction he has given.

Joshua is remembered as the one who, on the death of Moses, took command and completed the task of giving leadership to the tribes of Israel. Perhaps to comfort Joshua, who now had the responsibility for the children of Israel who didn't yet have a homeland, and perhaps to comfort that large body of people who had just lost their leader of more than forty years, the Lord spoke to Joshua and said: "As I was with Moses, so I will be with thee: I will not fail thee, nor forsake thee. Be strong and of a good courage: for unto this people shalt thou divide for an inheritance the land, which I sware unto their fathers to give them."

The Lord then spoke to Joshua by way of commandment: "Only be thou strong and very courageous, that thou mayest observe to do according to all the law, which Moses my servant commanded thee: turn not from it to the right hand or to the left, that thou mayest prosper whithersoever thou goest."

Then, speaking about the law given to Moses, the Lord added: "Observe to do according to all that is written therein: for then thou shalt make thy way prosperous, and then thou shalt have good success."

Finally, we have this last reiteration by the Lord of what he had previously said, to comfort and to remind Joshua of the relationship between the blessings of heaven and obedience to divine law: "Have not I commanded thee? Be strong and of a good courage; be not afraid, neither be thou dismayed: for the Lord thy God is with thee whithersoever thou goest." (Josh. 1:5–9.)

Joshua would need courage for what he had to do. He would need the Lord's help at every step. Here is a commitment of the Lord to provide that help. With faith in the Lord, Joshua could now go forward, knowing that the Lord would direct him in the way he should go. Joshua knew that his obedience would bring success, and although he did not know exactly how he would succeed, he now had confidence in the result.

The record tells us that the tribes of Israel moved to the Jordan River and encamped for three days, preparing to cross at a point near the city of Jericho. At that time Joshua gave his people this interesting counsel. He said, "Sanctify yourselves: for to morrow the Lord will do wonders among you." (Josh. 3:5.)

He knew the victory that would surely come would depend upon their willingness to do the will of the Lord. Then the Lord said unto Joshua, "This day will I begin to magnify thee in the sight of all Israel, that they may know that, as I was with Moses, so I will be with thee." (Josh. 3:7.)

Joshua now knew that the miracles of the Lord would continue, just as when Moses had been the leader of Israel. And so it was that when the feet of the priests bearing the ark of the covenant before the people touched the water of the Jordan, it dried up, "and all the Israelites passed over on dry ground." (Josh. 3:17.)

Soon after that, when Joshua was directed to destroy the city of Jericho that lay before them, the great walls of the city stood as an imposing and physically impossible barrier to Israel's success—or at least so it seemed. Not knowing the means, but assured as to the end, Joshua carried out the instructions he had been given by a messenger of the Lord. His commitment was to complete obedience. His concern was to do precisely as he was instructed, that the promise of the Lord would be fulfilled. The instructions no doubt seemed strange, but his faith in the outcome urged him on. The result, of course, was another in a long series of miracles experienced by the Israelites as they were led over many years by Moses, by Joshua, and by many other prophets who were committed to follow the commandments and the directives of the Lord.

As Joshua and his people approached Jericho, the instructions of the Lord were followed precisely and, according to the scriptural account, "the wall fell down flat, so that the people went up into the city, every man straight before him, and they took the city." (Josh. 6:20.)

The record states that after Israel had rested from the wars with their enemies, Joshua, who was now very old, called all Israel together. In his farewell address he reminded them they had been victorious because God had fought for them; but if they now ceased to serve the Lord and keep his law, they would be destroyed. He recalled how the Lord God of Israel had led

Abraham throughout Canaan and had "multiplied his seed." (Josh. 24:3.) He reminded them of how Jacob and his children had gone down into Egypt. He told of how the Lord had been with Moses and Aaron and had brought their fathers out of Egypt; how, in all of the battles and conquests, they had prevailed, adding this significant statement: "But not with thy sword, nor with thy bow." (Josh. 24:12.) The battles had not been won by superior weaponry. They had been led by the Lord to victory. He admonished them: "Fear the Lord, and serve him in sincerity and in truth: and put away the gods which your fathers served on the other side of the flood, and in Egypt; and serve ye the Lord." (Josh. 24:14.)

This great military and spiritual leader then urged a commitment, and made one himself and for his family: "Choose you this day whom ye will serve; . . . but as for me and my house, we will serve the Lord." (Josh. 24:15.)

Here was a great statement of full commitment of a man to God; of a prophet to the desires of the Lord; and of Joshua the man to his God, who had many times previously blessed his obedience. He was telling the Israelites that regardless of how they decided, he would do what he knew was right. He was saying that his decision to serve the Lord was independent of whatever they decided; that their actions would not affect his; that his commitment to do the Lord's will would not be altered by anything they or anyone else would do. Joshua was firmly in control of his actions and had his eyes fixed on the commandments of the Lord. He was committed to obedience.

Surely the Lord loves, more than anything else, an unwavering determination to obey his counsel. Surely the experiences of the great prophets of the Old Testament have been recorded to help us understand the importance of choosing the path of strict obedience. How pleased the Lord must have been when Abraham, after receiving direction to sacrifice his only son, Isaac, did as he was instructed, without question and without wavering.

The record states that God said unto Abraham: "Take now

thy son, thine only son Isaac, whom thou lovest, and get thee into the land of Moriah; and offer him there for a burnt offering upon one of the mountains which I will tell thee of." The next verse simply states: "And Abraham rose up early in the morning . . . and took . . . Isaac his son . . . and went unto the place of which God had told him." (Gen. 22:2–3.)

Years later, when Rebekah was asked if she would go with the servant of Abraham to become Isaac's wife, and no doubt knowing that the servant's mission had the blessing of the Lord, she simply said, "I will go." (Gen. 24:58.)

A generation after that, when Jacob was instructed to return to the land of Canaan, which meant leaving all for which he had worked many years, he called Rachel and Leah into the field where his flock was and explained what the Lord had said. The reply of Rachel was simple and straightforward and indicative of her commitment: "Whatsoever God hath said unto thee, do." (Gen. 31:16.)

We have, then, examples from the scriptures of how we should consider and evaluate the commandments of the Lord. If we choose to react like Joshua, Abraham, Rebekah, and Rachel, our response will be, simply, to go and do the thing that the Lord has commanded.

There is good reason to make our decision *now* to serve the Lord. On Sunday morning, when the complications and temptations of life are somewhat removed, and when we have the time and more of an inclination to take an eternal perspective, we can more clearly evaluate what will bring us the greatest happiness in life. We should decide now, in the light of the morning, how we will act when the darkness of night and when the storms of temptation arrive.

Chapter 27

TRUE RELIGION

*True religion is a devotion to God,
demonstrated by love and compassion for
fellowmen, coupled with unworldliness.*

Not long ago I read a report of an interview with a man of some national importance. In giving his views on a question of present-day concern, he made this comment: "I am not a religious man, but there was something about the circumstances of the proposed action that did not strike me as being right." His comment made me wonder why he associated religion with the social and political subject he was talking about, and it also made me wonder why he thought he was not a religious person. The answer to these queries, I suppose, lies in the definition of religion.

The word *religion* has no one generally accepted definition. Sometimes it is used in reference to worship, whether it be public or private, and sometimes to distinguish between things sacred and those that are profane or worldly. Belief in the immortality of the soul is a concept that is looked upon by some as religious, and one of the most common uses of the term is the belief in deity or deities—a worship of God. The word *religion* is often associated with the pursuit of what is commonly called salvation, and sometimes with revelation from a divine source.

Not long after the organization of the Church, Joseph Smith published answers to a long list of questions that had been asked of him. One of the questions was this: What are the fundamental principles of your religion? To that question, Joseph Smith replied: "The fundamental principles of our religion are the testimony of the Apostles and Prophets, concerning Jesus Christ, that He died, was buried, and rose again the third day, and ascended into heaven; and all other things which pertain to our religion are only appendages to it." (*History of the Church* 3:30.)

On many subjects we are often able to find definitions in the scriptures, but it is interesting to note that even though we think of the Bible as a religious treatise, the word *religion* does not appear in the Old Testament, and in the writings of the New Testament it is used on three occasions only. I would like to make reference to these three.

The first use of the word *religion* is by Paul as he presented his defense before King Agrippa. He said to Agrippa: "After the most straitest sect of our religion I lived a Pharisee." (Acts 26:5.) He was referring to the three sects of the Jews: the Pharisees, Sadducees, and Essenes. He said he lived a Pharisee—the sect of the three that was the strictest in religious practices. Paul was not talking about a religious creed or a belief, but rather the form of worship, because the Jews placed great stress on practice rather than doctrine—on ritualistic worship rather than a creed of belief.

The second use of the word *religion* was also by Paul, in writing to the Galatians. He made this statement: "For ye have heard of my conversation in time past in the Jews' religion, how that beyond measure I persecuted the church." (Gal. 1:13.) We well know of the persecutions inflicted by Paul upon those who followed Christ and professed to be Christians, and we wonder why he did these things. What caused him to take such a ruthless course?

Paul answers these questions by stating that he had practiced the religion of his fathers—a religion of iron rules, laws, and traditions inherited from his Hebrew lineage. These iron rules of

159

practice are what caused him to relentlessly persecute the followers of Christ. Thus, in writing to the Galatians, he referred to religion in the same manner as he did before King Agrippa, as rules of practice rather than doctrine or a creed of belief.

Now we come to the third instance in the New Testament of the use of the word *religion*. It is in the Epistle of James, written "to the twelve tribes which are scattered abroad" (James 1:1), probably meaning to all Israel. In this epistle he said: "If any man among you seem to be religious, and bridleth not his tongue, but deceiveth his own heart, this man's religion is vain." (James 1:26.) James seems to be using the term *religion* in the manner used by Paul, as being ritualistic or ceremonial—that if a man is ritualistic in this manner, yet fails to be guarded in what he says, his rituals are in vain.

James then very pointedly defines what he refers to as pure religion, as distinguished from forms of ritualistic worship and iron rules of practice as described by Paul. James said: "Pure religion and undefiled before God and the Father is this, To visit the fatherless and widows in their affliction, and to keep [oneself] unspotted from the world." (James 1:27.) The wording is simple and unpretentious, yet the meaning is profound and has deep significance. The words "visit the fatherless and widows" are a reminder that we should have compassion for our neighbor, our fellowmen. This is the teaching of the Master in his frequent reference to love. The Lord said: "Thou shalt love thy neighbour as thyself." (Matt. 22:39.) This is what James was expressing—a love for, and devotion to, God, by compassionate service to fellowmen. He used as examples the fatherless and the widows.

The second element of the definition of religion stated by James is to keep "unspotted from the world." To be unspotted from the world simply means being unworldly and free from the pollution of sin and unrighteousness. Paul also said something about this in his writing to the Romans: "Be not conformed to this world." (Rom. 12:2.)

In short, James tells us that true religion is devotion to God, demonstrated by love and compassion for fellowmen, coupled

160

with unworldliness. Such a statement seems too simple to be sufficient, but in its simplicity it speaks an important truth. Restated it may be said that true religion consists not only in refraining from evil (that is, remaining unspotted), but in deliberately and purposefully doing acts of kindness and service to others.

King Benjamin recognized this principle as he spoke to his people from the tower. He reminded them that he had spent his days in their service and said: "I do not desire to boast, for I have only been in the service of God. And behold, I tell you these things that ye may learn wisdom; that ye may learn that when ye are in the service of your fellow beings ye are only in the service of your God." (Mosiah 2:16–17.)

Matthew puts it this way: "Inasmuch as ye have done it unto one of the least of these my brethren, ye have done it unto me." (Matt. 25:40.)

The life of the Prophet Joseph Smith portrays these same attributes—service to friends, to his fellowmen, to all mankind, and to his God. It was during the last two hours of Joseph's life, confined behind bars in Carthage, that his close friend, President John Taylor, sang a song to cheer him on that melancholy occasion. The song has a number of verses commencing with helping the unfortunate and sharing a crust with one perishing for want of bread. These are some of the words:

A poor wayfaring man of grief
Had often crossed me on my way,
Who sued so humbly for relief
That I could never answer, Nay.

I had not power to ask his name;
Whither he went or whence he came;
Yet there was something in his eye
That won my love, I knew not why.

Once, when my scanty meal was spread,
He entered—not a word he spake!

161

Just perishing for want of bread;
I gave him all; he blessed it, brake.

And ate, but gave me part again;
Mine was an angel's portion then,
For while I fed with eager haste,
The crust was manna to my taste.

The verses continue to tell of a drink given to quench the thirst of a sufferer, clothing and rest for the naked and weary, caring for the injured and wounded, sharing the condemnation of a prisoner. Then the last verses recognize the appearance of the Master:

Then in a moment to my view,
The stranger started from disguise:
The tokens in his hands I knew,
The Savior stood before mine eyes.

He spake—and my poor name he named—
"Of me thou hast not been asham'd;
These deeds shall thy memorial be;
Fear not, thou didst them unto me."
(History of the Church 6:614–15.)

Poor, indeed, and destitute are those who disclaim being religious because they do not have sufficient love for their fellowmen to be concerned and have compassion. The Lord will say: "Inasmuch as ye did it not to one of the least of these, ye did it not to me. And these shall go away into everlasting punishment: but the righteous into life eternal." (Matt. 25:45–46.)

President Joseph F. Smith wrote these words many years ago: "Do not say that you are not naturally religious, and so make that an excuse for evil deeds and forbidden acts. . . . Be rather religious both in appearance and in reality, remembering what true religion means. Even as the testimony of Jesus is the spirit of prophecy, so is the possession of the knowledge that you love purity, righteousness, honesty, justice and well-doing, an indisputable evidence that you are naturally religious."

President Smith continued: "Search your hearts, and you will find deep down that you possess this knowledge. Then encourage its growth and development, to the gaining of your own salvation." ("Not Naturally Religious," *Improvement Era,* April 1906, p. 495.)

I pray we may serve our fellowmen and remain unspotted from worldly influences, so that we may be worthy to be considered truly religious and receive the approbation of the Lord.

Chapter 28

PUT YOUR
HAND TO THE PLOW

*Those who become disciples of the Master
and put their hands to the plow without
turning back prove themselves to be
worthy plowmen.*

Some time ago we were traveling through the air so high above the white clouds that they looked like a blanket of snow beneath us. The sky was blue, and the sun was shining, and then we commenced our descent for landing. As we came down through the clouds, a new scene came into view. The earth had been plowed for planting, and the sun was shining on the fields, some plowed in one direction and some in another. It made the earth appear as a great giant checkerboard. We came down and down and then, when within a few hundred feet on the ground, I saw a man laboring in the field, his hands fixed to a plow drawn by a horse. My thoughts turned to that closing verse in the ninth chapter of Luke in which the Master said: "No man, having put his hand to the plough, and looking back, is fit for the kingdom of God." (Luke 9:62.)

Christ made this statement as he traveled to Jerusalem. Three men had expressed their willingness to follow him and become his disciples. The first of these said to him: "Lord, I will follow thee whithersoever thou goest. And Jesus said unto him, Foxes have holes, and birds of the air have nests; but the Son of man hath not where to lay his head."

Jesus had no definite place of residence. He went from place to place teaching and doing good. It was necessary that the men who were called and set apart for the work should devote their time and attention and forgo worldly affairs. The work of the Master set the great example. The second man was also willing to follow. "But he said, Lord, suffer me first to go and bury my father. Jesus said unto him, Let the dead bury their dead: but go thou and preach the kingdom of God."

Does this statement sound severe? The Master made it clear that the work of the kingdom was to take precedence over all other things. Then the third man stepped forward and said: "Lord, I will follow thee; but let me first go bid them farewell, which are at home at my house."

None of the three were willing to follow Jesus without first returning to their worldly affairs. The answer of Jesus is one of the great aphorisms of biblical literature. "No man, having put his hand to the plough, and looking back, is fit for the kingdom of God." (Luke 9:57–62.)

In his teachings the Master used homely figures of speech, those having familiar, everyday character. The words "his hand to the plough" unfold a picture before us with which we are all familiar—a strong man with sinewy arms and a firm step, guiding the blade straight and true, his eyes intent upon the plow, looking ahead to the furrow to be cut. Hour after hour he toils, never looking backward except to see that the furrow is straight.

In addition to *plowing,* the Lord often mentioned the words *sowing* and *reaping.* He made mention of "reaping the harvest," and when that comes to our minds we think of a happy time and a time of rejoicing. The Lord said: "Lift up your eyes, and look on the fields; for they are white already to harvest. And he that reapeth receiveth wages, and gathereth fruit unto life eternal: that both he that soweth and he that reapeth may rejoice together." (John 4:35–36.)

Before there can be a reaping of the harvest, there must have been a sowing of the seed. When we think of sowing, our minds turn to the parable spoken by the Savior: "Behold, a sower went forth to sow; and when he sowed, some seeds fell by the way side, and the fowls came and devoured them up:

"Some fell upon stony places, where they had not much earth: and forthwith they sprung up, because they had no deepness of earth:

"And when the sun was up, they were scorched; and because they had no root, they withered away.

"And some fell among thorns; and the thorns sprung up, and choked them:

"But other fell into good ground, and brought forth fruit, some an hundredfold, some sixtyfold, and some thirtyfold." (Matthew 13:3–8.)

Sowing of seed is important; otherwise, there would be no harvest, and as stated in the parable, there must be good ground to bring forth a good harvest. Plowing must have been done before the sowing, or there would have been no seedbed.

Of all the work of the field, plow-work is the heaviest labor. It is primary and fundamental—it is pioneer toil. A seed may be dropped anywhere, and there is no resistance; but put the blade of the plow into the ground, and a thousand forces join to oppose the change. To disturb the conventional, to overturn the traditional, or to attempt to make changes in the deep-rooted way of doing things in the lives of individuals requires toil and sweat. The heaviest work in the kingdom of God is to turn the hard surface of the earth that has been baked in the sun or covered by the growth of nature. What a great change comes over land that has been cleared and plowed—row after row of evenly spaced furrows, the subsurface loosened and exposed to the sun and air and the rains from heaven, ready to be broken up and planted to seed. The wilderness is conquered and subdued.

Those who became disciples of the Master and put their hands to the plow without turning back proved themselves to be worthy plowmen. By turning over the old surfaces of tradition, they prepared the fields for the introduction and the spread of Christianity into the world.

We do not need to go back to the time of Christ, however, to find fields to plow. Fields exist today all over the world, and missionaries have been called and have put their hands to the plow. Furrows are being cut and seeds planted, and every day we see the results of the harvest.

And there is the field of education. Hundreds of plowmen are preparing the field for the harvest. They are teaching the principles of truth to our young men and young women in the Church Educational System.

Not many years ago we entered into the field of assisting those in need through the great welfare program. The plowshares were driven in and the soil turned over, disclosing the hidden possibilities of our arising to full stature in being our brothers' keeper. Men and women have joined in the labor of the field, and thousands have been helped and aided in the Lord's way, when in need.

We have in Church leadership great plowmen with firm hands and stout hearts—stake presidents, mission presidents, bishops, branch presidents, heads of priesthood quorums and auxiliary organizations—determined Saints who are toiling in their assigned fields. Close at home and in distant countries new lands are being broken up by these plowmen, and the subsurface exposed to the light of the gospel of Jesus Christ.

Is it hard work? Of course, but that which is worthwhile is seldom easy. As individuals, we have a responsibility to plow. Some accept the opportunity, but some shrink from the responsibility. Some of those who commence cut only a short furrow and then leave the field for what appears to be escape from the toil. Their plowshares are left to rust in the furrow.

Whatever the past may have been in our individual lives, it is gone. The future lies ahead, and we must face it with resolution. There is always a point from which we can begin. Even though we may have been faithful in the past, if we turn away, that faithfulness will profit us nothing. "No man, having put his hand to the plough, and looking back, is fit for the kingdom of God."

There is danger in looking backward. We must keep our eyes ahead in order to cut a straight furrow. When the plowman commences to look backward, he cuts a crooked furrow, and his work is spoiled. We cannot continue to walk forward when at the same time we are looking backward. It makes no difference what object or occasion causes us to look backward, the backward glance commences the backward turning, and may be the beginning of our disendowment in the kingdom of God.

Just as plowing requires an eye intent on the furrow to be made and is marred when one looks backward, so will they come short of exaltation who prosecute the work of God with a distracted attention or a divided heart. We may not see clearly the end of the furrow, but we dare not look back. Eternity stretches on ahead, challenging us to be faithful.

"And thus, if ye are faithful ye shall be laden with many sheaves, and crowned with honor, and glory, and immortality, and eternal life." (D&C 75:5.)

Chapter 29

A MORE
EXCELLENT WAY

*We need to be kinder, more gentle, more
forgiving, and slower to anger. We need to
love one another with the pure love of Christ.*

In an important message to the Latter-day Saints in Nauvoo
just one year before his tragic and untimely martyrdom, the
Prophet Joseph Smith said: "If we would secure and cultivate the
love of others, we must love others, even our enemies as well as
friends. . . . Christians should cease wrangling and contending
with each other, and cultivate the principles of union and friendship in their midst." (*History of the Church* 5:498–99.)

That is magnificent counsel today, even as it was in 1843. The
world in which we live, whether close to home or far away, needs
the gospel of Jesus Christ. It provides the only way the world will
ever know peace. We need to be kinder with one another, more
gentle and forgiving. We need to be slower to anger and more
prompt to help. We need to extend the hand of friendship and
resist the hand of retribution. In short, we need to love one
another with the pure love of Christ, with genuine charity and
compassion and, if necessary, shared suffering, for that is the way
God loved us.

In our worship services, we often sing a lovely hymn with

169

text written by Susan Evans McCloud. May I recall a few lines of that hymn for you:

> *Savior, may I learn to love thee,*
> *Walk the path that thou hast shown,*
> *Pause to help and lift another,*
> *Finding strength beyond my own. . . .*
>
> *Who am I to judge another*
> *When I walk imperfectly?*
> *In the quiet heart is hidden*
> *Sorrow that the eye can't see. . . .*
>
> *I would be my brother's keeper;*
> *I would learn the healer's art.*
> *To the wounded and the weary*
> *I would show a gentle heart.*
> *I would be my brother's keeper—*
> *Lord, I would follow thee.*
> —Hymns, *no. 220*

We need to walk more resolutely and more charitably the path that Jesus has shown. We need to "pause to help and lift another"; then surely we will find "strength beyond [our] own." If we would do more to learn the healer's art, there would be untold chances to use it, to touch the wounded and the weary and show to all a gentler heart. Yes, Lord, we should follow thee.

"A new commandment I give unto you," he said, "That ye love one another. . . . By this shall all men know that ye are my disciples, if ye have love one to another." (John 13:34–35.) This love that we should have for our brothers and sisters in the human family, and that Christ has for every one of us, is called charity or "the pure love of Christ." (Moro. 7:47.) It is the love that prompted the suffering and sacrifice of Christ's atonement. It is the highest pinnacle the human soul can reach and the deepest expression of the human heart.

We have a feeling of appreciation that our women's Relief

170

Society organization has always had as its theme "Charity Never Faileth." Charity encompasses all other godly virtues. It distinguishes both the beginning and the end of the plan of salvation. When all else fails, charity—Christ's love—will *not* fail. It is the greatest of all divine attributes.

Out of the abundance of his heart, Jesus spoke to the poor, the downtrodden, the widows, the little children; to farmers and fishermen, and those who tended goats and sheep; to strangers and foreigners, the rich, the politically powerful, as well as the unfriendly Pharisees and scribes. He ministered to the poor, the hungry, the deprived, the sick. He blessed the lame, the blind, the deaf, and other people with physical disabilities. He drove out the demons and evil spirits that had caused mental or emotional illness. He purified those who were burdened with sin. He taught lessons of love and repeatedly demonstrated unselfish service to others. All were recipients of his love. All were "privileged the one like unto the other, and none [were] forbidden." (2 Ne. 26:28.) These are all expressions and examples of his unbounded charity.

The world in which we live would benefit greatly if men and women everywhere would exercise the pure love of Christ, which is kind, meek, and lowly. It is without envy or pride. It is selfless because it seeks nothing in return. It does not countenance evil or ill will, nor rejoice in iniquity; it has no place for bigotry, hatred, or violence. It refuses to condone ridicule, vulgarity, abuse, or ostracism. It encourages diverse people to live together in Christian love regardless of religious belief, race, nationality, financial standing, education, or culture.

The Savior has commanded us to love one another as he has loved us; to clothe ourselves "with the bond of charity" (D&C 88:125), as he so clothed himself. We are called upon to purify our inner feelings, to change our hearts, to make our outward actions and appearance conform to what we say we believe and feel inside. We are to be true disciples of Christ.

As a young man, Brother Vern Crowley said he learned something of the crucial lesson the Prophet Joseph had taught

171

the early Saints in Nauvoo when he told them to "love others, even our enemies as well as friends." This is a good lesson for each of us.

After his father became ill, Vern Crowley took responsibility for running the family wrecking yard, although he was only fifteen years of age. Some customers occasionally took unfair advantage of the young man, and parts were disappearing from the lot overnight. Vern was angry and vowed to catch someone and make an example of that person. Vengeance would be his.

Just after his father had started to recover from his illness, Vern was making his rounds of the yard one night at closing time. It was nearly dark. In a distant corner of the property, he caught sight of someone carrying a large piece of machinery toward the back fence. He ran like a champion athlete and caught the young thief. His first thought was to take out his frustrations with his fists and then drag the boy to the front office and call the police. His heart was full of anger and vengeance. He had caught his thief, and he intended to get his just dues.

Out of nowhere, Vern's father came along, put his weak and infirm hand on his son's shoulder, and said, "I see you're a bit upset, Vern. May I handle this?" He then walked over to the young would-be thief and put his arm around his shoulder, looked him in the eye for a moment, and said, "Son, tell me, why are you doing this? Why were you trying to steal that transmission?" Then, with his arm still around the youth, he started walking toward the office, asking questions about the young man's car problems as they walked. By the time they had arrived at the office, the father said, "Well, I think your clutch is gone, and that's what's causing your problem."

In the meantime, Vern was fuming. *Who cares about his clutch?* he thought. *Let's call the police and get this over with.* But his father just kept talking. "Vern, get him a clutch. Get him a throwout bearing, too. And get him a pressure plate. That should take care of it." The father handed the parts to the young man who had attempted the robbery and said, "Take these. And here's the transmission, too. You don't have to steal, young man. Just ask for it. There's a way out of every problem. People are willing to help."

Brother Vern Crowley said he learned an everlasting lesson in love that day. The young man came back to the lot often. Voluntarily, month by month, he paid for all of the parts Vic Crowley had given him, including the transmission. During those visits, he asked Vern why his father was the way he was and why he did what he did. Vern told him something of their Latter-day Saint beliefs and how much his father loved the Lord and loved people. Eventually the would-be thief was baptized. Vern later said, "It's hard now to describe the feelings I had and what I went through in that experience. I too was young. I had caught my crook. I was going to extract the utmost penalty. But my father taught me a different way."

A different way? A better way? A higher way? A more excellent way? Oh, how the world could benefit from such a magnificent lesson. As Moroni declares: "Wherefore, whoso believeth in God might with surety hope for a better world, . . . in the gift of his Son hath God prepared a more excellent way." (Ether 12:4, 11.)

President David O. McKay once said: "The peace of Christ does not come by seeking the superficial things of life, neither does it come except as it springs from the individual's heart. Jesus said to his disciples: 'Peace I leave with you, my peace I give unto you: not as the world giveth, give I unto you.'" (*Gospel Ideals* [Salt Lake City: Improvement Era, 1953], pp. 39–40.)

In all the realms of daily living and in a world with so many needs, we should so live that one day we will hear the King of kings say to us: "For I was an hungred, and ye gave me meat: I was thirsty, and ye gave me drink: I was a stranger, and ye took me in: Naked, and ye clothed me: I was sick, and ye visited me: I was in prison, and ye came unto me."

And if we should have occasion to say, "Lord, when saw we thee an hungred, and fed thee? or thirsty, and gave thee drink? When saw we thee a stranger, and took thee in? or naked, and clothed thee? Or when saw we thee sick, or in prison, and came unto thee?" I am certain we will hear this reply:

"Inasmuch as ye have done it unto one of the least of these my brethren, ye have done it unto me." (Matt. 25:35–40.)

We need a more peaceful world, growing out of more peaceful families and neighborhoods and communities. To secure and cultivate such peace, as the Prophet Joseph taught us, "we must love others, even our enemies as well as our friends." The world needs the gospel of Jesus Christ. Those who are filled with the love of Christ do not seek to force others to do better; they inspire others to do better—indeed, inspire them to the pursuit of God. We need to extend the hand of friendship. We need to be kinder, more gentle, more forgiving, and slower to anger. We need to love one another with the pure love of Christ. May this be our course and our desire.

Chapter 30

ETHICS ALONE
IS NOT SUFFICIENT

*We have a need for ethics, but true religion
includes the truths of ethics
and goes far beyond.*

Not long ago one of our national publications reported an extensive study of some conditions plaguing our modern society, conditions that give us great concern. Crimes of violence are increasing at an alarming rate. There is disrespect for law and order, civil disobedience, expanded use of drugs and barbiturates, increase in venereal diseases, and an accelerating divorce rate. The upward trend in crimes of violence, petty thefts, burglary, gambling, and protests against standards that have long prevailed as acceptable is alarming.

Can we say that because news media are filled with such accounts, there is a universal and basic social change in thinking and conduct? Can we believe that because there are some who have no regard for the law or the rights of others, this represents a new concept of right and wrong? Although we cannot hide our heads in the sand and disregard present-day problems, I for one have not lost faith in my fellowmen.

Among our modern youth are some who take great delight in attracting attention by pursuing a course against the conventional. By a misguided sense of direction, this vocal minority often campaigns for a new freedom disassociated from any sense of responsibility. For every one of these, there are thousands of young people who want to live right and do right. They have the desire to take their place in a responsible society and to live under a code of high morality. We are proud of them. These are the great hope of the future. I only wish their good works and their aspirations could receive the same "equal time" as is allotted to those of opposing political philosophies.

What makes the difference? What causes people to travel divergent courses on moral issues? Is it because of a difference in belief as to whether a thing is right or wrong, or is it a total disregard for the right?

We teach little children the difference between right and wrong, and a conscience awakens in them. There seems to be in each of God's children this monitoring device we call a conscience, which tracks our thoughts and actions and raises cautions when there is contemplation of the improper, unconventional, or immoral. Often merely living with others teaches us the difference between right and wrong. Something is lacking in the experience of an adult who must be taken into custody and punished or restrained for violating the rights of others. But again, these people are in the minority. I think we would agree that most people have a sense of right and wrong and a sincere desire to follow the right. They have an understanding of moral responsibility. Sometimes we refer to this as ethics, the science of moral duty or ideal human character.

I believe that most persons follow a strict code of ethics. They are governed by this great ethical rule: So live as to invoke the best in others and therefore in yourself. Surely this is commendable and would enhance relationships in our complex society if everyone had a sincere feeling of such moral responsibility.

Ethical theory is the basis for righteous government and for the formulation of fair and equitable jurisprudence. It is the basis for all moral, social, and economic systems.

We would agree that by following a strict code of moral ethics, society would reach a high state of perfection and many of the present-day problems would be solved, but is ethics alone sufficient to attain our goals in life? To those who have no belief in life after mortality, ethics may be sufficient to fulfill the requirements of conduct and responsibility. There may be some who believe in a life hereafter, yet feel that ethics is sufficient for salvation. Can this be true without our also living the other commandments of God?

There is a great difference between ethics and religion. There is a distinction between one whose life is based on mere ethics and one who lives a truly religious life. We have a need for ethics, but true religion includes the truths of ethics and goes far beyond. True religion has its roots in belief in a supreme being. Christian religion is based upon belief in God the Eternal Father and in his Son Jesus Christ and in the word of the Lord as contained in scripture. Religion also goes beyond theology. It is more than just belief in Deity; it is the practice of that belief. James E. Talmage said, "One may be deeply versed in theological lore, and yet be lacking in religious and even in moral character. If theology be theory then religion is practise; if theology be precept religion is example." (*Articles of Faith* [Salt Lake City: Deseret Book, 1981], pp. 5–6.)

True religion to the Christian is demonstrated by a real belief in God and the realization that we are responsible to him for our acts and conduct. A person who lives such religion is willing to live the principles of the gospel of Christ and walk uprightly before the Lord in all things according to his revealed law. This brings to an individual a sense of peace and freedom from confusion in life and gives an assurance of eternal life hereafter. The Lord said, "Man shall not live by bread alone, but by every word that proceedeth out of the mouth of God." (Matt. 4:4.) A code of morals is not wholly sufficient. For the same reason that we cannot be saved by bread alone, we cannot be saved by a code of ethics.

In order to be effective in one's life, religion must be a vibrant influence. It must be an influence that becomes a part of one's thinking and conduct. There is purpose in our sojourn in mortality. We are placed here for a definite reason, in accordance with God's great plan. We read in Genesis the story of the creation: "And the Lord God said, Behold, the man is become as one of us, to know good and evil." (Gen. 3:22.)

To learn the difference between good and evil is one of the great purposes of mortal life, yet we are given our freedom of choice with the promise of eternal blessings if we obey the laws of God.

True religious faith teaches us that there are certain principles that must be accepted and obeyed. We must have faith in God the Eternal Father and in his Son, Jesus Christ, and his atoning sacrifice. This must be followed by repentance from all sin; then baptism by immersion, after the example of the Savior, by one having authority; and the laying on of hands for the gift of the Holy Ghost. Other things are necessary, including a contrite spirit, a humble heart, obedience to the ordinances and principles of the gospel, and faithfulness to the end. This encompasses the choosing of right over wrong, following good, and abstaining from evil.

Ethics alone will not accomplish all these things for us, but an active religion will add to ethics the principles and ordinances of the gospel, which, if obeyed, will open the doors of eternal salvation, provided such religion is ordained of God and not of man's creation. I bear witness to you that the Church established by Christ and taken from the earth because of the apostasy of men has been restored in these latter days in the same manner as foretold by the prophets of old and by the other statements of scripture, and that God has spoken to his servants in our day and is now speaking. The Church of Jesus Christ of Latter-day Saints invites all persons to listen to the story of the restoration of the gospel, the story of a religion vibrant and vital in the lives of thousands of persons of faith, testimony, and devotion to the principles of the gospel taught by the Church of Christ.

The troubles of the world often expressed in screaming headlines should remind us to seek for the peace that comes from living the simple principles of the gospel of Christ. The vociferous minorities will not unsettle our peace of soul if we love our fellow beings and have faith in the atoning sacrifice of the Savior and the quiet assurance he gives of life everlasting. Where do we find such faith in a troubled world? The Lord said, "Ask, and it shall be given you; seek, and ye shall find; knock, and it shall be opened unto you. For every one that asketh receiveth; and he that seeketh findeth; and to him that knocketh it shall be opened." (Luke 11:9–10.)

Chapter 31

DEVELOPING
OUR SPIRITUALITY

*Developing spirituality is accomplished only
through deliberate effort and by calling upon
God and keeping his commandments.*

President Wilford Woodruff once had a remarkable experience to which I would like to refer. He first publicly mentioned the incident at general conference in October of 1880. Sixteen years later he gave further details in a discourse delivered at the Weber Stake conference, and his remarks were published in the *Deseret Weekly.* In the 1880 conference President Woodruff told of dreams he had after the death of the Prophet Joseph Smith in which he conversed with the Prophet many times. He then related another dream in which he talked with Brigham Young, and this is what he said about it:

> On one occasion, I saw Brother Brigham and Brother Heber ride in [a] carriage ahead of the carriage in which I rode when I was on my way to attend conference; and they were dressed in the most priestly robes. When we arrived at our destination I asked Prest. Young if he would preach to us. He said, "No, I have finished my testimony in the flesh I shall not talk to this people any more. But (said he) I have come to see you; I have come to watch over you, and to see what the people are doing. Then (said he) I want you to teach the people—and I want you

180

to follow this counsel yourself—that they must labor and so live as to obtain the Holy Spirit, for without this you cannot build up the kingdom; without the spirit of God you are in danger of walking in the dark, and in danger of failing to accomplish your calling as apostles and as elders in the church and kingdom of God. And, said he, Brother Joseph taught me this principle." (*Journal of Discourses*, 21:318.)

At the Weber Stake conference, President Woodruff went on to say of that experience essentially what I want to say today: "Every man and woman in this Church should labor to get that Spirit. We are surrounded by these evil spirits that are at war against God and against everything looking to the building up of the kingdom of God; and we need this Holy Spirit to enable us to overcome these influences." (*Deseret Weekly*, November 7, 1896, p. 643.)

Continuing his discourse, President Woodruff told of his missionary experiences. He said:

In the time of the apostasy in Kirtland . . . the Spirit of God said to me, "You choose a partner and go straight to Fox Islands." Well, I knew no more what was on Fox Islands than what was on Kolob. But the Lord told me to go, and I went. I chose Jonathan H. Hale, and he went with me. . . . Through the blessings of God I brought nearly a hundred from there up to Zion, at the time the Saints were driven out of Missouri into Illinois.

So it has been all through my life. If I have undertaken to do anything, and the Lord has wanted me to do something else, He has had to tell me. When we were sent to England, we were sent by revelation. I went into the Staffordshire potteries with Brother Alfred Cordon. We were doing a splendid work, baptizing almost every night, and I thought it was the finest mission I ever was on. I went into the town of Hanley one night, and attended meeting in a large hall, which was filled to overflowing. The Spirit of the Lord came upon me and said that that was the last meeting I should hold with that people for many days. I told the people that that was the last meeting I should be with them. After the meeting, they asked me where

181

I was going. I told them I did not know. In the morning I asked the Lord what He wanted of me. He merely said, "Go to the south." I got into the stage and rode eighty miles. The first man's house I stopped at was John Benbow's in Herefordshire. In half an hour after I entered the house I knew exactly why the Lord had sent me. There was a people there who had been praying for the ancient order of things. They were waiting for the Gospel as it was taught by Christ and His Apostles. The consequence was, the first thirty days after I got there I baptized six hundred of those people. In eight month's labor in that country I brought eighteen hundred into the Church. Why? Because there was a people prepared for the Gospel, and the Lord sent me there to do that work. I have always had to give God the glory for everything good that has happened to me; for I have realized by what power it came. . . .

I refer to these things because I want you to get the same Spirit. All the Elders of Israel, whether abroad or at home, need that Spirit. . . . This is the Spirit that we must have to carry out the purposes of God on the earth. We need that more than any other gift. . . . We are in the midst of enemies, in the midst of darkness and temptation, and we need to be guided by the Spirit of God. We should pray to the Lord until we get the Comforter. This is what is promised to us when we are baptized. It is the spirit of light, of truth, and of revelation and can be with all of us at the same time. (*Deseret Weekly,* 7 Nov. 1896, p. 643.)

Developing spirituality and attuning ourselves to the highest influences of godliness is not an easy matter. It takes time and frequently involves a struggle. It will not happen by chance, but is accomplished only through deliberate effort and by calling upon God and keeping his commandments.

The Apostle Paul spent much of his life teaching and encouraging spirituality in the then far-flung missions of the world. He frequently used terminology from the sports, games, and athletic contests. He said that a Saint successfully keeping the commandments is like an athlete winning his contest: comparable degrees of training, exertion, obedience to the rules, self-discipline, and the will to win are involved. To the Corinthians he wrote words to this effect: "You know (do you not?) that at the sports all the runners run the race, though only one wins the prize. Like them, run to win! Now every athlete goes into strict training. They do it to win a perishable wreath, but our wreath will last forever. For my part I run with a clear goal before me." (See 1 Cor. 9:24–26.)

Along this same line he said to Timothy, his beloved young friend and missionary companion: "I have fought a good fight, I have finished my course, I have kept the faith: Henceforth there is laid up for me a crown of righteousness, which the Lord, the righteous judge, shall give me at that day: and not to me only; but unto all them also that love his appearing." (2 Tim. 4:7–8.)

Taking the athletic contest to what was in ancient times the ultimate experience—a hand-to-hand battle to the death—Paul wrote this statement regarding such physical combat:

"Put on the whole armour of God, that ye may be able to stand against the wiles of the devil. For we wrestle not against flesh and blood, but against principalities, against powers, against the rulers of the darkness of this world, against spiritual wickedness in high places. Wherefore take unto you the whole armour of God, that ye may be able to withstand in the evil day, and having done all, to stand.

"Stand therefore, having your loins girt about with truth, and having on the breastplate of righteousness; and your feet shod with the preparation of the gospel of peace; above all, taking the shield of faith, wherewith ye shall be able to quench all the fiery darts of the wicked.

"And take the helmet of salvation, and the sword of the Spirit, which is the word of God: Praying always with all prayer and supplication in the Spirit, and watching thereunto with all perseverance and supplication for all saints." (Eph. 6:11–18.)

The Prophet Joseph Smith did not speak in such athletic or military terms, but he has given us perhaps the clearest statement of all on the need to become spiritual, as well as the time and patience that we must recognize are part of the process. He said:

"We consider that God has created man with a mind capable of instruction, and a faculty which may be enlarged in proportion to the heed and diligence given to the light communicated from heaven to the intellect; and that the nearer man approaches perfection, the clearer are his views, and the greater his enjoyments, till he has overcome the evils of his life and lost every desire for sin; and like the ancients, arrives at that point of faith where he is wrapped in the power and glory of his Maker, and is caught up to dwell with Him. But we consider that this is a station to which no man ever arrived in a moment." (*History of the Church* 2:8.)

Part of our difficulty as we strive to acquire spirituality is the feeling that there is much to do and we are falling far short. Perfection is something yet ahead for every one of us; but we can capitalize on our strengths, begin where we are, and seek after the happiness that can be found in pursuing the things of God. We should remember the Lord's counsel: "Wherefore, be not weary in well-doing, for ye are laying the foundation of a great work. And out of small things proceedeth that which is great. Behold, the Lord requireth the heart and a willing mind; and the willing and obedient shall eat the good of the land of Zion in these last days." (D&C 64:33–34.)

It has always been encouraging to me that the Lord said it is the "willing and obedient [who] shall eat the good of the land of Zion in these last days." Each of us can be willing and obedient. If the Lord had said the perfect shall eat the good of the land of Zion in these last days, I suppose some of us would be discouraged and give up.

The Prophet Joseph said, "Happiness is the object and design of our existence; and will be the end thereof, if we pursue the path that leads to it; and this path is virtue, uprightness, faithfulness, holiness, and keeping all the commandments of God." (*History of the Church* 5:134–35.)

The place to begin is here. The time to start is now. The length of our stride need be but one step at a time. God, who has designed our happiness, will lead us along even as little children, and we will by that process approach perfection.

None of us has attained perfection or the zenith of spiritual growth that is possible in mortality. Every person can and must make spiritual progress. The gospel of Jesus Christ is the divine plan for that spiritual growth eternally. It is more than a code of ethics. It is more than an ideal social order. It is more than positive thinking about self-improvement and determination. The gospel is the saving power of the Lord Jesus Christ with his priesthood and sustenance and with the Holy Spirit. With faith in the Lord Jesus Christ and obedience to his gospel, a step at a time improving as we go, pleading for strength, improving our attitudes and our ambitions, we will find ourselves successfully in the fold of the Good Shepherd. That will require discipline and training and exertion and strength. But as the Apostle Paul said, "I can do all things through Christ which strengtheneth me." (Philip. 4:13.)

A modern-day revelation makes this promise: "Put your trust in that Spirit which leadeth to do good—yea, to do justly, to walk humbly, to judge righteously; and this is my Spirit. Verily, verily, I say unto you, I will impart unto you of my Spirit, which shall enlighten your mind, which shall fill your soul with joy; and then shall ye know, or by this shall you know, all things whatsoever you desire of me, which are pertaining unto things of righteousness, in faith believing in me that ye shall receive." (D&C 11:12–14.)

Chapter 32

"AN UNDERSTANDING HEART"

We need more understanding in our
relationships with one another. Hatred tears
down, but understanding builds up.

For forty years David had reigned over Israel, and as his life was drawing to a close, he appointed his son Solomon as his successor to the throne. Solomon inherited the great kingdom that had been secured by the military genius of his father. The empire extended from the Mediterranean Sea to the Euphrates River, and from the Syrian desert to the Red Sea. It became the task of this young man, then less than twenty years of age, to weld this great empire into a unity.

As his last will and testament, King David called Solomon to his side and, knowing the great task that would fall on the shoulders of this youth, said to him: "I go the way of all the earth: be thou strong therefore, and shew thyself a man; and keep the charge of the Lord thy God, to walk in his ways, to keep his statutes, and his commandments, and his judgments, and his testimonies, as it is written in the law of Moses, that thou mayest prosper in all that thou doest, and whithersoever thou turnest thyself." (1 Kgs. 2:2–3.)

After this, King David died and Solomon commenced the administration of the affairs of the kingdom, and the record makes this comment: "And Solomon loved the Lord, walking in the statutes of David his father." (1 Kgs. 3:3.)

Not long after Solomon became king, he went to a nearby city to offer sacrifices, and while he was there an event occurred that had a significant effect upon his life and reign. The scriptures tell us that "in Gibeon the Lord appeared to Solomon in a dream by night: and God said, Ask what I shall give thee." (1 Kgs. 3:5.)

What a grave and serious question this would present to anyone, to have the Lord say, "Ask what I shall give thee."

If you could have one wish, what would it be? There are so many things we wish for as we go through life. I presume nearly every child who has read the story of the *Arabian Nights* has wished for a lamp like the one Aladdin had, which when rubbed would summon the genie who would do the bidding regardless of the request made of him. Wishing is not just the pastime of children. Most of us have made wishes. We have wished for health and wealth, success, happiness, wisdom, a better job, a new car, a diamond ring, a magic carpet, to be like someone else, to have that which is not within reach, to be given the easy way instead of the path of toil and hardship—and a thousand and one other things.

We might wonder what went through Solomon's mind when the Lord said to him, "Ask what I shall give thee." No doubt his mind traveled the same course as ours would travel if the question were to be asked of us. Solomon had just ascended the throne, and although he had ambitions for the future, he must have had some fears and anxieties. The fact that he was a king would give him the right to most things a person would want, yet a king has many of the same problems and the desires of those who are not of royalty. The question would be no less difficult for a king than it would be for one of a more lowly station.

Solomon must have had many thoughts cross his mind. We might assume he thought of asking for a long life. Others have done so when such a question has been put to them. A long life would have given him the opportunity to complete the ambitions of his father to build and extend the empire. We cling to life;

we wish for more time to accomplish the many things opportunity places in our pathway. Time is usually all too short when we think of the things we want to do and the lessons we wish to learn before the time comes for us to return home. No doubt Solomon thought of these things as he viewed the extent of his great empire, yet this was not foremost in his mind.

He might have thought of riches and wealth. Another king before him had made such a wish. In mythology the Greek god Bacchus gave to King Midas any wish he could name because he had rescued one of Bacchus's followers. King Midas asked that all he touched be turned into gold, but he soon learned the utter uselessness of this wish when food and drink became gold at the touch of his lips. Most of the early sovereigns of the ancient world have been known for their great accumulation of the treasures of the earth. Wealth has always been associated with power. One might assume that a king would have a desire for wealth in order to spread his influence and prestige and to extend the borders of his kingdom. But Solomon did not ask for riches or wealth.

The reign of Solomon's father, David, over Israel was one of wars with the Philistines and the Syrians and many other campaigns. These conquests gave Israel the foremost place among the nations between the Euphrates and Egypt. To maintain this superiority, Solomon was challenged at the beginning of his reign to maintain a large standing army to provide for the defense of the empire. He organized a cavalry force of twelve thousand men, and equipped the royal stables with four thousand stalls to maintain the fourteen hundred royal chariots. He fortified Jerusalem and other cities for protection against invasion and to preserve the trade routes for commerce. Israel's fighting strength consisted of about three hundred thousand men.

With all of these problems facing him, Solomon might have asked the Lord to give him power over his enemies, for he had enemies from without the empire, and he had personal enemies within. But the young king asked for none of these things. His answer to the Lord was simple and direct:

"Thou hast shewed unto thy servant David my father great mercy, according as he walked before thee in truth, and in righteousness, and in uprightness of heart with thee; and thou hast kept for him this great kindness, that thou hast given him a son to sit on his throne, as it is this day.

"And now, O Lord my God, thou hast made thy servant king instead of David my father: and I am but a little child: I know not how to go out or come in. And thy servant is in the midst of thy people which thou hast chosen, a great people, that cannot be numbered nor counted for multitude. Give therefore thy servant an understanding heart to judge thy people, that I may discern between good and bad: for who is able to judge this thy so great a people?" The young king did not ask for material things of the world, but a spiritual gift—an understanding heart.

"And the speech pleased the Lord, that Solomon had asked this thing. And God said unto him, Because thou hast asked this thing, and hast not asked for thyself long life; neither hast asked riches for thyself, nor hast asked the life of thine enemies; but hast asked for thyself understanding to discern judgment; behold, I have done according to thy words: lo, I have given thee a wise and an understanding heart; so that there was none like thee before thee, neither after thee shall any arise like unto thee.

"And I have also given thee that which thou hast not asked, both riches, and honour: so that there shall not be any among the kings like unto thee all thy days." (1 Kgs. 3:6–13.)

If the Lord was pleased because of what Solomon had asked of him, surely he would be pleased with each of us if we had the desire to acquire an understanding heart. This must come from conscious effort coupled with faith and firm determination. An understanding heart results from the experiences we have in life if we keep the commandments of God. Jesus said: "Thou shalt love the Lord thy God with all thy heart, and with all thy soul, and with all thy mind. This is the first and great commandment. And the second is like unto it, Thou shalt love thy neighbour as thyself." (Matt. 22:37–39.)

To love one's neighbor is noble and inspiring, whether the

189

neighbor is one who lives close by or, in a broader sense, a fellow being of the human race. It stimulates the desire to promote happiness, comfort, interest, and the welfare of others. It creates understanding. The ills of the world would be cured by understanding. Wars would cease and crime would disappear. The scientific knowledge now being wasted in the world because of the distrust of men and nations could be diverted to bless mankind. Atomic energy will destroy unless used for peaceful purposes by understanding hearts.

We need more understanding in our relationships with one another, in business and in industry, between management and labor, between government and the governed. We need understanding in that most important of all social units, the family; understanding between children and parents and between husband and wife. Marriage would bring happiness, and divorce would be unknown if there were understanding hearts. Hatred tears down, but understanding builds up.

Our prayer could well be as was Solomon's: "Lord, give me an understanding heart."

SOURCES OF TALKS

The messages in this book, with minor editing, have been taken from the following sources. The talks were given in general conferences except as noted.

1. "What Manner of Men Ought Ye to Be?," *Ensign*, May 1994, 64.
2. "Jesus, the Very Thought of Thee," *Ensign*, May 1993, 63–65.
3. "Come unto Me," *Ensign*, Nov. 1990, 17–18.
4. "The Beacon in the Harbor of Peace," *Ensign*, Nov. 1992, 18–19.
5. "Where, Then, Is Hope?," *Improvement Era*, Dec. 1970, 115–17.
6. "Where Is Peace?," *Improvement Era*, Dec. 1966, 1104–5.
7. "The Temptations of Christ," *Ensign*, Nov. 1976, 17–19.
8. "Master, the Tempest Is Raging," *Ensign*, Nov. 1984, 33–35.
9. "That We May Be One," *Ensign*, May 1976, 105–6.
10. "The Church Is for All People," *Ensign*, Nov. 1989, 75–77, from a talk given at a single adults satellite broadcast, Feb. 26, 1989.
11. "The Gospel: A Global Faith," *Ensign*, Nov. 1991, 18–19.
12. "Secretly a Disciple," *Improvement Era*, Dec. 1960, 948–49.
13. "All Are Alike unto God," *Ensign*, June 1979, 72–74, from a talk given at a fourteen-stake fireside at Brigham Young University, Feb. 4, 1979.
14. "The Golden Thread of Choice," *Ensign*, Nov. 1989, 17–18.

15. "Make Us Thy True Undershepherds," *Ensign*, Sept. 1986, 6–9; from a talk given at a priesthood leadership meeting, Apr. 4, 1986.

16. "An Anchor to the Souls of Men," *Ensign*, Oct. 1993, 70–73, from a talk given at a Church Educational System fireside, Feb. 7, 1993.

17. "God Will Have a Tried People," *Ensign*, May 1980, 24–25.

18. "What Is True Greatness?," *Ensign*, Sept. 1987, 70–72, from a talk given at Brigham Young University, Feb. 10, 1987.

19. "Parents' Concern for Children," *Ensign*, Nov. 1983, 63–65.

20. "Blessed from On High," *Ensign*, Nov. 1988, 59–61.

21. "The Opening and Closing of Doors," *Ensign*, Nov. 1987, 55, 59–60.

22. "Gospel Imperatives," *Ensign*, June 1967, 101–3.

23. "The Pharisee and the Publican," *Ensign*, May 1984, 64–66.

24. "The Lord's Touchstone," *Ensign*, Nov. 1986, 34–35.

25. "Am I a 'Living' Member?," *Ensign*, May 1987, 16–18.

26. "Our Commitment to God," *Ensign*, Nov. 1982, 57–58.

27. "True Religion," *Ensign*, Nov. 1978, 11–13.

28. "Put Your Hand to the Plow," *Improvement Era*, June 1961, 398–99.

29. "A More Excellent Way," *Ensign*, May 1992, 61–63.

30. "Ethics Alone Is Not Sufficient," *Ensign*, Dec. 1969, 96–97.

31. "Developing Our Spirituality," *Ensign*, May 1979, 24–26.

32. "An Understanding Heart," *Ensign*, June 1962, 442–43.

INDEX

193